Jean Louis,
C'est avec très grand
plaisir que je partage ces
avec toi, with love. Eric
X-Mas '07

W9-BEX-617

Thich Nhat Hanh

Translated by Mobi Ho

With Eleven Drawings by Vo-Dinh Mai

The Miracle
of Mindfulness

*An Introduction to the Practice
of Meditation*

 Beacon Press   Boston

Beacon Press
25 Beacon Street
Boston, Massachusetts 02108-2892
www.beacon.org

Beacon Press books
are published under the auspices of
the Unitarian Universalist Association of Congregations.

09 08 07   11 10 9

The Library of Congress catalogued the previous
paperback edition as follows:

Nhãt Hanh, Thích.
    The miracle of mindfulness.
    Translation of Phép la cua su tinh thuc.
        ISBN 0-8070-1232-7 (cloth)
        ISBN 0-8070-1239-4 (paper)
    1. Meditation (Buddhism)   2. Buddhist meditations.
I. Title.
BQ5618.V5N4813   1987   294.3'433   87-42582

Contents

Translator's Preface

The Miracle of Mindfulness was originally written in Vietnamese as a long letter to Brother Quang, a main staff member of the School of Youth for Social Service in South Vietnam in 1974. Its author, the Buddhist monk Thich Nhat Hanh, had founded the School in the 1960s as an outgrowth of "engaged Buddhism." It drew young people deeply committed to acting in a spirit of compassion. Upon graduation, the students used the training they received to respond to the needs of peasants caught in the turmoil of the war. They helped rebuild bombed villages, teach children, set up medical stations, and organize agricultural cooperatives.

The workers' methods of reconciliation were often misunderstood in the atmosphere of fear and mistrust engendered by the war. They persistently refused to support either armed party and believed that both sides were but the reflection of one reality, and the true enemies were not people, but ideology, hatred, and ignorance. Their stance threatened those engaged in the conflict, and in the first years of the School, a series of attacks were carried out against the students. Several were kidnapped and murdered. As the war dragged on, even after the Paris Peace Accords were signed in 1973, it seemed at times impossible not to succumb to exhaustion and bitterness. Continuing to work in a spirit of love and understanding required great courage.

From exile in France, Thich Nhat Hanh wrote to Brother Quang to encourage the workers during this dark time. Thay Nhat Hanh ("Thay," the form of address for Vietnamese monks, means "teacher") wished to remind them of the essential discipline of following one's breath to nourish and maintain calm mindfulness, even in the midst of the most difficult circumstances. Because Brother Quang and the students were his colleagues and friends, the spirit of this long letter that became *The Miracle of Mindfulness* is personal and direct. When Thay speaks here of village paths, he speaks of paths he had actually walked with Brother Quang. When he mentions the bright eyes of a young child, he mentions the name of Brother Quang's own son.

I was living as an American volunteer with the Vietnamese Buddhist Peace Delegation in Paris when Thay was writing the letter. Thay headed the delegation, which served as an overseas liaison office for the peace and reconstruction efforts of the Vietnamese Buddhists, including the School of Youth for Social Service. I remember late evenings over tea, when Thay explained sections of the letter to delegation members and a few close friends. Quite naturally, we began to think of other people in other countries who might also benefit from the practices described in the book.

Thay had recently become acquainted with young Buddhists in Thailand who had been inspired by the witness of engaged Buddhism in Vietnam. They too wished to act in a spirit of awareness and reconciliation to help avert the armed conflict erupting in Thailand, and they wanted to know how to work without being overcome by anger and discouragement. Several of them spoke English, and we discussed translating Brother Quang's letter. The idea of a translation took on a special poignancy when the confiscation of Buddhist publishing houses in Vietnam made the project of printing the letter as a small book in Vietnam impossible.

I happily accepted the task of translating the book into English. For nearly three years, I had been living with the Vietnamese Buddhist Peace Delegation, where day and night I was immersed in the lyrical sound of the Vietnamese language. Thay·had been my "formal" Vietnamese teacher; we had slowly read through some of his earlier books, sentence by sentence. I had thus acquired a rather unusual vocabulary of Vietnamese Buddhist terms. Thay, of course, had been teaching me far more than language during those three years. His presence was a constant gentle reminder to return to one's true self, to be awake by being mindful.

As I sat down to translate *The Miracle of Mindfulness*, I remembered the episodes during the past years that had nurtured my own practice of mindfulness. There was the time I was cooking furiously and could not find a spoon I'd set down amid a scattered pile of pans and ingredients. As I searched here and there, Thay entered the kitchen and smiled. He asked, "What is Mobi looking for?" Of course, I answered, "The spoon! I'm looking for a spoon!" Thay answered, again with a smile, "No, Mobi is looking for Mobi."

Thay suggested I do the translation slowly and steadily, in order to maintain mindfulness. I translated only two pages a day. In the evenings, Thay and I went over those pages, changing and correcting words and sentences. Other friends provided editorial assistance. It is difficult to describe the actual experience of translating his words, but my awareness of the feel of pen and paper, awareness of the position of my body and of my breath enabled me to see most clearly the mindfulness with which Thay had written each word. As I watched my breath, I could see Brother Quang and the workers of the School of Youth for Social Service. More than that, I began to see that the words held the same personal and lively directness for any reader because they had been written in mindfulness and lovingly directed to real people. As I continued to translate, I could see an expanding community—the School's workers, the young Thai Buddhists, and many other friends throughout the world.

When the translation was completed we typed it, and Thay printed a hundred copies on the tiny offset machine squeezed into the delegation's bathroom. Mindfully addressing each copy to friends in many countries was a happy task for delegation members.

Since then, like ripples in a pond, *The Miracle of Mindfulness* has traveled far. It has been translated into several other languages and has been printed or distributed on every continent in the world. One of the joys of being the translator has been to hear from many people who have discovered the book. I once met someone in a bookstore who knew a student who had taken a copy to friends in the Soviet Union. And recently, I met a young Iraqi student in danger of being deported to his homeland, where he faces death for his refusal to fight in a war he believes cruel and senseless; he and his mother have both read *The Miracle of Mindfulness* and are practicing awareness of the breath. I have learned, too, that proceeds from the Portuguese edition are being used to assist poor children in Brazil. Prisoners, refugees, health-care workers, educators, and artists are among those whose lives have been touched by this little book. I often think of *The Miracle of Mind-*

fulness as something of a miracle itself, a vehicle that continues to connect lives throughout the world.

American Buddhists have been impressed by the natural and unique blending of Theravada and Mahayana traditions, characteristic of Vietnamese Buddhism, which the book expresses. As a book on the Buddhist path, *The Miracle of Mindfulness* is special because its clear and simple emphasis on basic practice enables any reader to begin a practice of his or her own immediately. Interest in the book, however, is not limited to Buddhists. It has found a home with people of many different religious traditions. One's breath, after all, is hardly attached to any particular creed.

Those who enjoy this book will likely be interested in other books by Thich Nhat Hanh which have been translated into English. His books in Vietnamese, including short stories, novels, essays, historical treatises on Buddhism and poetry, number in the dozens. While several of his earlier books in English are no longer in print, more recent works available in translation include *A Guide to Walking Meditation, Being Peace,* and *The Sun My Heart.*

Denied permission to return to Vietnam, Thich Nhat Hanh spends most of the year living in Plum Village, a community he helped found in France. There, under the guidance of the same Brother Quang to whom *The Miracle of Mindfulness* was originally addressed years ago, community members tend hundreds of plum trees. Profits from the sales of their fruit are used to assist hungry children in Vietnam. In addition, Plum Village is open every summer to visitors from around the world who wish to spend a month of mindfulness and meditation. In recent years, Thich Nhat Hanh has also made annual visits to the United States and Canada to conduct week-long retreats organized by the Buddhist Peace Fellowship.

I would like to express special gratitude to Beacon Press for having the vision to print this new edition of *The Miracle of Mindfulness*. I hope that each new person whom it reaches will sense that the book is addressed as personally to him or her as it was to Brother Quang and the workers of the School of Youth for Social Service.

Mobi Ho
August 1987

The Miracle of
Mindfulness

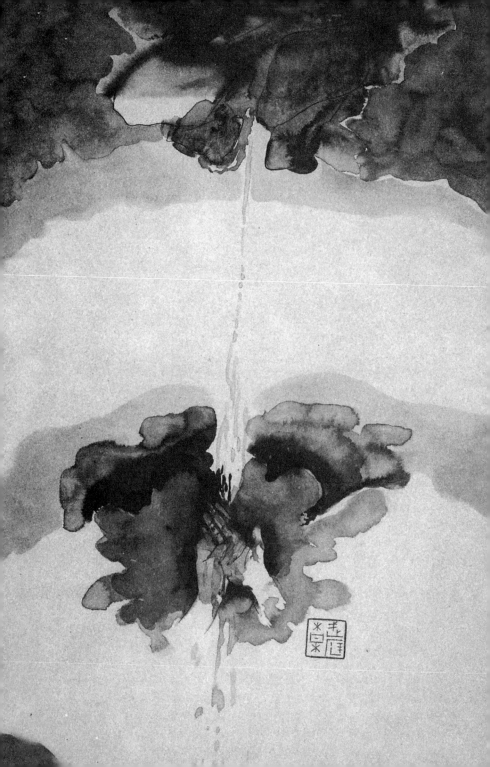

One ❀

The Essential Discipline

Yesterday Allen came over to visit with his son Joey. Joey has grown so quickly! He's already seven years old and is fluent in French and English. He even uses a bit of slang he's picked up on the street. Raising children here is very different from the way we raise children at home. Here parents believe that "freedom is necessary for a child's development." During the two hours that Allen and I were talking, Allen had to keep a constant eye on Joey. Joey played, chattered away, and interrupted us, making it impossible to carry on a real conversation. I gave him several picture books for children but he barely glanced at them before tossing them aside and interrupting our conversation again. He demands the constant attention of grown-ups.

Later, Joey put on his jacket and went outside to play with a neighbor's child. I asked Allen, "Do you find family life easy?" Allen

1

didn't answer directly. He said that during the past few weeks, since the birth of Ana, he had been unable to sleep any length of time. During the night, Sue wakes him up and—because she is too tired herself—asks him to check to make sure Ana is still breathing. "I get up and look at the baby and then come back and fall asleep again. Sometimes the ritual happens two or three times a night."

"Is family life easier than being a bachelor?" I asked. Allen didn't answer directly. But I understood. I asked another question: "A lot of people say that if you have a family you're less lonely and have more security. Is that true?" Allen nodded his head and mumbled something softly. But I understood.

Then Allen said, "I've discovered a way to have a lot more time. In the past, I used to look at my time as if it were divided into several parts. One part I reserved for Joey, another part was for Sue, another part to help with Ana, another part for household work. The time left over I considered my own. I could read, write, do research, go for walks.

"But now I try not to divide time into parts anymore. I consider my time with Joey and Sue as my own time. When I help Joey with his homework, I try to find ways of seeing his time as my own time. I go through his lesson with him, sharing his presence and finding ways to be interested in what we do during that time. The time for him becomes my own time. The same with Sue. The remarkable thing is that now I have unlimited time for myself!"

2

Allen smiled as he spoke. I was surprised. I knew that Allen hadn't learned this from reading any books. This was something he had discovered for himself in his own daily life.

Washing the dishes to wash the dishes

Thirty years ago, when I was still a novice at Tu Hieu Pagoda, washing the dishes was hardly a pleasant task. During the Season of Retreat when all the monks returned to the monastery, two novices had to do all the cooking and wash the dishes for sometimes well over one hundred monks. There was no soap. We had only ashes, rice husks, and coconut husks, and that was all. Cleaning such a high stack of bowls was a chore, especially during the winter when the water was freezing cold. Then you had to heat up a big pot of water before you could do any scrubbing. Nowadays one stands in a kitchen equipped with liquid soap, special scrubpads, and even running hot water which makes it all the more agreeable. It is easier to enjoy washing the dishes now. Anyone can wash them in a hurry, then sit down and enjoy a cup of tea afterwards. I can see a machine for washing clothes, although I wash my own things out by hand, but a dishwashing machine is going just a little too far!

While washing the dishes one should only be washing the dishes, which means that while washing the dishes one should be completely aware of the fact that one is washing the dishes. At first glance, that might seem a little silly:

why put so much stress on a simple thing? But that's precisely the point. The fact that I am standing there and washing these bowls is a wondrous reality. I'm being completely myself, following my breath, conscious of my presence, and conscious of my thoughts and actions. There's no way I can be tossed around mindlessly like a bottle slapped here and there on the waves.

The cup in your hands

In the United States, I have a close friend named Jim Forest. When I first met him eight years ago, he was working with the Catholic Peace Fellowship. Last winter, Jim came to visit. I usually wash the dishes after we've finished the evening meal, before sitting down and drinking tea with everyone else. One night, Jim asked if he might do the dishes. I said, "Go ahead, but if you wash the dishes you must know the way to wash them." Jim replied, "Come on, you think I don't know how to wash the dishes?" I answered, "There are two ways to wash the dishes. The first is to wash the dishes in order to have clean dishes and the second is to wash the dishes in order to wash the dishes." Jim was delighted and said, "I choose the second way—to wash the dishes to wash the dishes." From then on, Jim knew how to wash the dishes. I transferred the "responsibility" to him for an entire week.

If while washing dishes, we think only of the cup of tea that awaits us, thus hurrying to get the dishes out of the way as if they were a nuisance, then we are not "washing the dishes to wash the dishes." What's more, we are not alive during the time we are washing the dishes. In fact we are completely incapable of realizing the miracle of life while standing at the sink. If we can't wash the dishes, the chances are we won't be able to drink our tea either. While drinking the cup of tea, we will only be thinking of other things, barely aware of the cup in our hands. Thus we are sucked away into the future —and we are incapable of actually living one minute of life.

Eating a tangerine

I remember a number of years ago, when Jim and I were first traveling together in the United States, we sat under a tree and shared a tangerine. He began to talk about what we would be doing in the future. Whenever we thought about a project that seemed attractive or inspiring, Jim became so immersed in it that he literally forgot about what he was doing in the present. He popped a section of tangerine in his mouth and, before he had begun chewing it, had another slice ready to pop into his mouth again. He was hardly aware he was eating a tangerine. All I had to say was, "You ought to eat the tangerine section you've already taken." Jim was startled into realizing what he was doing.

It was as if he hadn't been eating the tangerine at all. If he had been eating anything, he was "eating" his future plans.

A tangerine has sections. If you can eat just one section, you can probably eat the entire tangerine. But if you can't eat a single section, you cannot eat the tangerine. Jim understood. He slowly put his hand down and focused on the presence of the slice already in his mouth. He chewed it thoughtfully before reaching down and taking another section.

Later, when Jim went to prison for activities against the war, I was worried about whether he could endure the four walls of prison and sent him a very short letter: "Do you remember the tangerine we shared when we were together? Your being there is like the tangerine. Eat it and be one with it. Tomorrow it will be no more."

The Essential Discipline

More than thirty years ago, when I first entered the monastery, the monks gave me a small book called "The Essential Discipline for Daily Use," written by the Buddhist monk Doc The from Bao Son pagoda, and they told me to memorize it. It was a thin book. It couldn't have been more than 40 pages, but it contained all the thoughts Doc The used to awaken his mind while doing any task. When he woke up in the morning, his first thought was, "Just awakened, I hope that every person will attain great awareness and see in complete clarity." When he washed his hands, he used this thought to place himself in mindfulness: "Washing my hands, I hope that every person will have pure hands to receive reality." The book is comprised entirely of such sentences. Their goal was to help the beginning practitioner take hold of his own consciousness. The Zen Master Doc The helped all of us young novices to practice, in a relatively easy way, those things which are taught in the Sutra of Mindfulness. Each time you put on your robe, washed the dishes, went to the bathroom, folded your mat, carried buckets of water, or brushed your teeth, you could use one of the thoughts from the book in order to take hold of your own consciousness.

The Sutra of Mindfulness* says, "When walking, the practitioner must be conscious that he is walking. When sitting, the practitioner must be conscious that he is sitting. When lying down, the practitioner must be conscious that he is lying down. . . . No matter what position one's body is in, the practitioner must be conscious of that position. Practicing thus, the practitioner lives in direct and constant mindfulness of the body . . ." The mindfulness of

_____

*In the Sutras, Buddha usually teaches that one should use one's breath in order to achieve Concentration. The Sutra which speaks about the use of your breath to maintain mindfulness is the Anapanasati Sutra. This Sutra was translated and commentated on by a Vietnamese Zen Master of Central Asian origin named Khuong Tang Hoi, around the beginning of the Third Century A.D. Anapana means breath and sati means mindfulness. Tang Hoi translated it as "Guarding the Mind." The Anapanasati Sutra, that is, is the sutra on using one's breath to maintain mindfulness. The Sutra on Breath to Maintain Mindfulness is the 118th Sutra in the Majhima Nikaya collection of sutras and it teaches 16 methods of using one's breath.

7

the positions of one's body is not enough, however. We must be conscious of each breath, each movement, every thought and feeling, everything which has any relation to ourselves.

But what is the purpose of the Sutra's instruction? Where are we to find the time to practice such mindfulness? If you spend all day practicing mindfulness, how will there ever be enough time to do all the work that needs to be done to change and to build an alternative society? How does Allen manage to work, study Joey's lesson, take Ana's diapers to the laundromat, and practice mindfulness at the same time?

Two ✿

The Miracle Is
to Walk on Earth

Allen said that since he's begun to consider Joey's and Sue's time as his own, he has "unlimited time." But perhaps he has it only in principle. Because there are doubtless times when Allen forgets to consider Joey's time as his own time while going over Joey's homework with him, and thus Allen may lose that time. Allen might hope for the time to pass quickly, or he may grow impatient because that time seems wasted to him, because it isn't his own time. And so, if he really wants "unlimited time," he will have to keep alive the realization that "this is my time" throughout the time he's studying with Joey. But during such times, one's mind is inevitably distracted by other thoughts, and so if one really wants to keep one's consciousness alive (from now on I'll use the term "mindfulness" to refer to keeping one's consciousness alive to the present reality), then one must practice right now in

11

one's daily life, not only during meditation sessions.

When you are walking along a path leading into a village, you can practice mindfulness. Walking along a dirt path, surrounded by patches of green grass, if you practice mindfulness you will experience that path, the path leading into the village. You practice by keeping this one thought alive: "I'm walking along the path leading into the village." Whether it's sunny or rainy, whether the path is dry or wet, you keep that one thought, but not just repeating it like a machine, over and over again. Machine thinking is the opposite of mindfulness. If we're really engaged in mindfulness while walking along the path to the village, then we will consider the act of each step we take as an infinite wonder, and a joy will open our hearts like a flower, enabling us to enter the world of reality.

I like to walk alone on country paths, rice plants and wild grasses on both sides, putting each foot down on the earth in mindfulness, knowing that I walk on the wondrous earth. In such moments, existence is a miraculous and mysterious reality. People usually consider walking on water or in thin air a miracle. But I think the real miracle is not to walk either on water or in thin air, but to walk on earth. Every day we are engaged in a miracle which we don't even recognize: a blue sky, white clouds, green leaves, the black, curious eyes of a child—our own two eyes. All is a miracle.

Sitting

Zen Master Doc The says that when sitting in meditation, one should sit upright, giving birth to this thought, "Sitting here is like sitting on the Bodhi spot." The Bodhi spot is where Lord Buddha sat when he obtained Enlightenment. If any person can become a Buddha, and the Buddhas are all those countless persons who have obtained enlightenment, then many have sat on the very spot I sit on now. Sitting on the same spot as a Buddha gives rise to happiness and sitting in mindfulness means itself to have become a Buddha. The poet Nguyen Cong Tru experienced the same thing when he sat down on a certain spot, and suddenly saw how others had sat on the same spot countless ages ago, and how in ages to come others would also come to sit there:

On the same spot I sit today
Others came, in ages past, to sit.
One thousand years, still others will come.
Who is the singer, and who the listener?

That spot and the minutes he spent there became a link in eternal reality.

But active, concerned people don't have time to spend leisurely, walking along paths of green grass and sitting beneath trees. One must prepare projects, consult with the neighbors, try to resolve a million difficulties; there is hard work to do. One must deal with every kind of hardship, every moment keeping one's atten-

13

tion focused on the work, alert, ready to handle the situation ably and intelligently.

You might well ask: Then how are we to practice mindfulness?

My answer is: keep your attention focused on the work, be alert and ready to handle ably and intelligently any situation which may arise —this is mindfulness. There is no reason why mindfulness should be different from focusing all one's attention on one's work, to be alert and to be using one's best judgment. During the moment one is consulting, resolving, and dealing with whatever arises, a calm heart and self-control are necessary if one is to obtain good results. Anyone can see that. If we are not in control of ourselves but instead let our impatience or anger interfere, then our work is no longer of any value.

Mindfulness is the miracle by which we master and restore ourselves. Consider, for example: a magician who cuts his body into many parts and places each part in a different region—hands in the south, arms in the east, legs in the north, and then by some miraculous power lets forth a cry which reassembles whole every part of his body. Mindfulness is like that —it is the miracle which can call back in a flash our dispersed mind and restore it to wholeness so that we can live each minute of life.

Taking hold of one's breath

Thus mindfulness is at the same time a means and an end, the seed and the fruit. When we practice mindfulness in order to build up concentration, mindfulness is a seed. But mindfulness itself is the life of awareness: the presence of mindfulness means the presence of life, and therefore mindfulness is also the fruit. Mindfulness frees us of forgetfulness and dispersion and makes it possible to live fully each minute of life. Mindfulness enables us to live.

You should know how to breathe to maintain mindfulness, as breathing is a natural and extremely effective tool which can prevent dispersion. Breath is the bridge which connects life to consciousness, which unites your body to your thoughts. Whenever your mind becomes scattered, use your breath as the means to take hold of your mind again.

Breathe in lightly a fairly long breath, conscious of the fact that you are inhaling a deep breath. Now breathe out all the breath in your lungs, remaining conscious the whole time of the exhalation. The Sutra of Mindfulness teaches the method to take hold of one's breath in the following manner: "Be ever mindful you breathe in and mindful you breathe out. Breathing in a long breath, you know, 'I am breathing in a long breath.' Breathing out a long breath, you know, 'I am breathing out a long breath.' Breathing in a short breath, you know, 'I am breathing in a short breath.' Breathing out a short breath, you know, 'I am breathing out a short breath.'"

"Experiencing a whole breath-body, I shall breathe in," thus you train yourself. "Experiencing the whole breath-body, I shall breathe out," thus you train yourself. "Calming the

15

activity of the breath-body, I shall breathe in,"
thus you train yourself. "Calming the activity
of the breath-body, I shall breathe out," thus
you train yourself.

In a Buddhist monastery, everyone learns
to use breath as a tool to stop mental dispersion
and to build up concentration power. Concentration power is the strength which comes
from practicing mindfulness. It is the concentration which can help one obtain the Great
Awakening. When a worker takes hold of his
own breath, he has already become awakened.
In order to maintain mindfulness throughout a
long period, we must continue to watch our
breath.

It is autumn here and the golden leaves falling one by one are truly beautiful. Taking a
10-minute walk in the woods, watching my
breath and maintaining mindfulness, I feel
refreshed and restored. Like that, I can really
enter into a communion with each leaf.

Of course, walking alone on a country path,
it is easier to maintain mindfulness. If there's a
friend by your side, not talking but also watching his breath, then you can continue to maintain mindfulness without difficulty. But if
the friend at your side begins to talk, it becomes
a little more difficult.

If, in your mind, you think, "I wish this
fellow would quit talking, so I could concentrate," you have already lost your mindfulness.
But if you think, instead, "If he wishes to talk,
I will answer, but I will continue in mindfulness,

aware of the fact that we are walking along this path together, aware of what we say, I can continue to watch my breath as well."

If you can give rise to that thought, you will be continuing in mindfulness. It is harder to practice in such situations than when you are alone, but if you continue to practice nonetheless, you will develop the ability to maintain much greater concentration. There is a line from a Vietnamese folk song that says: "Hardest of all is to practice the Way at home, second in the crowd, and third in the pagoda." It is only in an active and demanding situation that mindfulness really becomes a challenge!

Counting one's breath and following one's breath

In the meditation sessions I recently began for non-Vietnamese, I usually suggest various methods that I myself have tried, methods that are quite simple. I suggest to beginners the method of "Following the length of the breath." The student lies, back down, on the floor. Then I invite all of the participants to gather around so I can show them a few simple points:

1) Although inhaling and exhaling are the work of the lungs, and take place in the chest area, the stomach area also plays a role. The stomach rises with the filling of the lungs. At the beginning of the breath the stomach begins to push out. But after inhaling about two-thirds of the breath, it starts to lower again.

2) Why? Between your chest and stomach there is a muscuiar membrane, the diaphragm. When you breathe in correctly the air fills the lower part of the lungs first, before the upper lungs fill with air, the diaphragm pushes down on the stomach, causing the stomach to rise. When you have filled your upper lungs with air, the chest pushes out and causes the stomach to lower again.

3) That is why, in former times, people spoke of the breath as originating at the navel and terminating at the nostrils.

For beginners, lying down to practice breathing is very helpful. The important thing is to guard against making too much of an effort: too great an effort can be dangerous for the lungs, especially when the lungs are weak from many years of incorrect breathing. In the beginning, the practitioner should lie on his or her back on a thin mat or blanket, the two arms loosely at the sides. Don't prop your head on a pillow. Focus your attention on your exhalation and watch how long it is. Measure it slowly by counting in your mind: 1, 2, 3. . . After several times, you will know the "length" of your breath: Perhaps it is 5. Now try to extend the exhalation for one more count (or 2) so that the exhalation's length becomes 6 or 7. Begin to exhale counting from 1 to 5. When you reach 5, rather than immediately inhaling as

18

before, try to extend the exhalation to 6 or 7. This way you will empty your lungs of more air. When you have finished exhaling, pause for an instant to let your lungs take in fresh air on their own. Let them take in just as much air as they want without making· any effort. The inhalation will normally be "shorter" than the exhalation. Keep a steady count in your mind to measure the length of both. Practice several weeks like this, remaining mindful of all your exhalations and inhalations while lying down. (If you have a clock with a loud tick you can use it to help you keep track of the length of your inhalation and exhalation.)

Continue to measure your breath while walking, sitting, standing, and especially whenever you are outdoors. While walking, you might use your steps to measure your breath. After a month or so, the difference between the length of your exhalation and inhalation will lessen, gradually evening out until they are of equal measure. If the length of your exhalation is 6, the inhalation will also be 6.

If you feel at all tired while practicing, stop at once. But even if you do not feel tired, don't prolong the practice of long, equal breaths beyond short periods of time—10 to 20 breaths are enough. The moment you feel the least fatigue, return your breathing to normal. Fatigue is an excellent mechanism of our bodies and the best advisor as to whether one should rest or continue. In order to measure your breath you can count—or use a rhythmic phrase that you like. (If the length of your breath is

6, you might use instead of numbers, the six words, "My heart is now at peace." If the length is 7 you might use, "I walk on the new green earth." A Buddhist might say, "I take refuge in the Buddha." For a Christian it could be "Our Father who art in heaven." When you are walking, each step should correspond to one word.

Quiet breathing

Your breath should be light, even, and flowing, like a thin stream of water running through the sand. Your breath should be very quiet, so quiet that a person sitting next to you cannot hear it. Your breathing should flow gracefully, like a river, like a watersnake crossing the water, and not like a chain of rugged mountains or the gallop of a horse. To master our breath is to be in control of our bodies and minds. Each time we find ourselves dispersed and find it difficult to gain control of ourselves by different means, the method of watching the breath should always be used.

The instant you sit down to meditate, begin watching your breath. At first breathe normally, gradually letting your breathing slow down until it is quiet, even, and the lengths of the breaths are fairly long. From the moment you sit down to the moment your breathing has become deep and silent, be conscious of everything that is happening in yourself.

As the Buddhist Sutra of Mindfulness says: "Breathing in a long breath, you know, 'I am breathing in a long breath.' Breathing out a long breath, the practitioner knows, 'I am breathing out a long breath.' Breathing in a short breath, you know, 'I am breathing in a short breath.' Breathing out a short breath, you know, 'I am breathing out a short breath.' Experiencing the whole breath-body, I shall breathe in." Thus you train yourself. "Experiencing the whole breath-body, I shall breathe out." Thus you train yourself. "Calming the activity of the breath-body, I shall breathe in." Thus you train yourself. "Calming the activity of the breath-body, I shall breathe out." Thus you train yourself.

After about 10 to 20 minutes, your thoughts will have quieted down like a pond on which not even a ripple stirs.

Counting your breath

Making your breath calm and even is called the method of following one's breath. If it seems hard at first, you can substitute the method of counting your breath. As you breathe in, count 1 in your mind, and as you breathe out, count 1. Breathe in, count 2. Breathe out, count 2. Continue through 10, then return to 1 again. This counting is like a string which attaches your mindfulness to your breath. This exercise is the beginning point in the process of becoming continuously conscious of your breath. Without mindfulness, however, you will quickly lose count. When the count is lost, simply return to 1 and keep trying until you can keep the count correctly. Once you can truly focus your attention on the counts, you have reached the point at which you can begin to abandon the counting method and begin to concentrate solely on the breath itself.

. In those moments when you are upset or dispersed and find it difficult to practice mindfulness, return to your breath: Taking hold of your breath is itself mindfulness. Your breath is the wondrous method of taking hold of your consciousness. As one religious community says in its rule, "One should not lose oneself in mind-dispersion or in one's surroundings. Learn to practice breathing in order to regain control of body and mind, to practice mindfulness, and to develop concentration and wisdom."

Every act is a rite

Suppose there is a towering wall from the top of which one can see vast distances—but there is no apparent means to climb it, only a thin piece of thread hanging over the top and coming down both sides. A clever person will tie a thicker string onto one end of the thread, walk over to the other side of the wall, then pull on the thread bringing the string to the other side. Then he will tie the end of the string to a strong rope and pull the rope over. When the rope has reached the bottom of one side and is secured on the other side, the wall can be easily scaled.

Our breath is such a fragile piece of thread. But once we know how to use it, it can become a wondrous tool to help us surmount situations

22

which would otherwise seem hopeless. Our breath is the bridge from our body to our mind, the element which reconciles our body and mind and which makes possible one-ness of body and mind. Breath is aligned to both body and mind and it alone is the tool which can bring them both together, illuminating both and bringing both peace and calm.

Many persons and books discuss the immense benefits that result from correct breathing. They report that a person who knows how to breathe is a person who knows how to build up endless vitality: breath builds up the lungs, strengthens the blood, and revitalizes every organ in the body. They say that proper breathing is more important than food. And all of these statements are correct.

Years ago, I was extremely ill. After several years of taking medicine and undergoing medical treatment, my condition was unimproved. So I turned to the method of breathing and, thanks to that, was able to heal myself.

Breath is a tool. Breath itself is mindfulness. The use of breath as a tool may help one obtain immense benefits, but these cannot be considered as ends in themselves. These benefits are only the by-products of the realization of mindfulness.

In my small class in meditation for non-Vietnamese, there are many young people. I've told them that if each one can meditate an hour each day that's good, but it's nowhere near enough. You've got to practice meditation when you walk, stand, lie down, sit, and work, while washing your hands, washing the dishes, sweeping the floor, drinking tea, talking to friends, or whatever you are doing: "While washing the dishes, you might be thinking about the tea afterwards, and so try to get them out of the way as quickly as possible in order to sit and drink tea. But that means that you are incapable of living during the time you are washing the dishes. When you are washing the dishes, washing the dishes must be the most important thing in your life. Just as when you're drinking tea, drinking tea must be the most important thing in your life. When you're using the toilet, let that be the most important thing in your life." And so on. Chopping wood is meditation. Carrying water is meditation. Be mindful 24 hours a day, not just during the one hour you may allot for formal meditation or reading scripture and reciting prayers. Each act must be carried out in mindfulness. Each act is a rite, a ceremony. Raising your cup of tea to your mouth is a rite. Does the word "rite" seem too solemn? I use that word in order to jolt you into the realization of the life-and-death matter of awareness.

Three 🌸

A Day of Mindfulness

Every day and every hour, one should practice mindfulness. That's easy to say, but to carry it out in practice is not. That's why I suggest to those who come to the meditation sessions that each person should try hard to reserve one day out of the week to devote entirely to their practice of mindfulness. In principle, of course every day should be your day, and every hour your hour. But the fact is that very few of us have reached such a point. We have the impression that our family, place of work, and society rob us of all our time. So I urge that everyone set aside one day each week. Saturday, perhaps.

If it is Saturday, then Saturday must be entirely your day, a day during which you are completely the master. Then Saturday will be the lever that will lift you to the habit of practicing mindfulness. Every worker in a peace or service community, no matter how urgent its work, has the right to such a day, for without it we will lose ourselves quickly in a life full of worry and action, and our responses will become increasingly useless. Whatever the day chosen, it can be considered as the day of mindfulness.

To set up a day of mindfulness, figure out a way to remind yourself at the moment of waking that this day is your day of mindfulness. You might hang something on the ceiling or on the wall, a paper with the word "mindfulness" or a pinebranch—anything that will suggest to you as you open your eyes and see it that today is your day of mindfulness. Today is your day. Remembering that, perhaps you can feel a smile which affirms that you are in complete mindfulness, a smile that nourishes that perfect mindfulness.

While still lying in bed, begin slowly to follow your breath—slow, long, and conscious breaths. Then slowly rise from bed (instead of turning out all at once as usual), nourishing mindfulness by every motion. Once up, brush your teeth, wash your face, and do all your morning activities in a calm and relaxing way, each movement done in mindfulness. Follow your breath, take hold of it, and don't let your thoughts scatter. Each movement should be done calmly. Measure your steps with quiet, long breaths. Maintain a half smile.

Spend at least a half hour taking a bath. Bathe slowly and mindfully, so that by the time you have finished, you feel light and refreshed. Afterwards, you might do household work such as washing dishes, dusting and wiping off the tables, scrubbing the kitchen floor, arranging books on their shelves. Whatever the tasks, do them slowly and with ease, in mindfulness. Don't do any task in order to get it over with. Resolve to do each job in a relaxed way, with all your attention. Enjoy and be one with your work. Without this, the day of mindfulness will be of no value at all. The feeling that any task is a nuisance will soon disappear if it is done in mindfulness. Take the example of the Zen Masters. No matter what task or motion they undertake, they do it slowly and evenly, without reluctance.

For those who are just beginning to practice, it is best to maintain a spirit of silence throughout the day. That doesn't mean that on the day of mindfulness, you shouldn't speak at all. You can talk, you can even go ahead and sing, but if you talk or sing, do it in complete mindfulness of what you are saying or singing, and keep talking and singing to a minimum. Naturally, it is possible to sing and practice mindfulness at the same time, just as long as one is conscious of the fact that one is singing and aware of what one is singing. But be warned that it is much easier, when singing or talking, to stray from mindfulness if your meditation strength is still weak.

At lunchtime, prepare a meal for yourself. Cook the meal and wash the dishes in mindfulness. In the morning, after you have cleaned and straightened up your house, and in the afternoon, after you have worked in the garden or watched clouds or gathered flowers, prepare a pot of tea to sit and drink in mindfulness. Allow yourself a good length of time to do this. Don't drink your tea like someone who gulps down a cup of coffee during a workbreak. Drink your tea slowly and reverently, as if it is the axis on which the whole earth revolves—slowly, evenly, without rushing toward the future. Live the actual moment. Only this actual moment is life. Don't be attached to the future. Don't worry about things you have to do. Don't think about getting up or taking off to do anything. Don't think about "departing."

> Be a bud sitting quietly in the hedge
> Be a smile, one part of wondrous existence
> Stand here. There is no need to depart.
> This homeland is as beautiful as the homeland of
>   our childhood
> Do not harm it, please, and continue to sing . . .
> ("Butterfly Over the Field of Golden Mustard Flowers")

In the evening, you might read scripture and copy passages, write letters to friends, or do anything else you enjoy outside of your normal duties during the week. But whatever you do, do it in mindfulness. Eat only a little for the evening meal. Later, around 10 or 11 o'clock, as you sit in meditation, you will be able to sit more easily on an empty stomach. Afterwards you might take a slow walk in the fresh night air, following your breath in mindfulness and measuring the length of your breaths by your steps. Finally, return to your room and sleep in mindfulness.

Somehow we must find a way to allow each worker a day of mindfulness. Such a day is crucial. Its effect on the other days of the week is immeasurable. Ten years ago, thanks to such a day of mindfulness, Chu Van and our other sisters and brothers in the Tiep Hien Order were able to guide themselves through many difficult times. After only three months of observing such a day of mindfulness once a week, I know that you will see a significant change in your life. The day of mindfulness will begin to penetrate the other days of the week, enabling you to eventually live seven days a week in mindfulness. I'm sure you agree with me on the day of mindfulness's importance!

Four ❁

The Pebble

Why should you meditate? First of all, because each of us needs to realize total rest. Even a night of sleep doesn't provide total rest. Twisting and turning, the facial muscles tense, all the while dreaming—hardly rest! Nor is lying down rest when you still feel restless and twist and turn. Lying on your back, with your arms and legs straight but not stiff, your head unsupported by a pillow—this is a good position to practice breathing and to relax all the muscles; but this way it is also easier to fall asleep. You cannot go as far in meditation lying down as by sitting. It is possible to find total rest in a sitting position, and in turn to advance deeper in meditation in order to resolve the worries and troubles that upset and block your consciousness.

Among our workers in Vietnam there are many who can sit in the lotus position, the left foot placed on the right thigh and the right foot placed on the left thigh. Others can sit in the half lotus, the left foot placed on the right thigh, or the right foot placed on the left thigh. In our meditation class in Paris, there are people who do not feel comfortable in either of the above two positions and so I have shown them how to sit in the Japanese manner, the knees bent, resting on their two legs. By placing a pillow beneath one's feet, it is possible to sit that way for more than an hour and a half. Even so, anyone can learn to sit in the half lotus, though at the beginning it may be somewhat painful. But after a few weeks of practice, the position gradually becomes quite comfortable. During the initial period, when the pain can be bothersome, alternate the position of the legs or change to another sitting position. If one sits in the lotus or half-lotus position, it is necessary to use a cushion to sit on so that both knees touch the floor. The three points of bodily contact with the floor created by this position provide an extremely stable position.

Keep your back straight. This is very important. The neck and head should be aligned with the spinal column; they should be straight but not stiff or wood-like. Keep your eyes focused a yard or two in front of you. If you can, maintain a half smile.

Now begin to follow your breath and to relax all of your muscles. Concentrate on keeping your spinal column straight and on following your breath. As for everything else, let it go. Let go of everything. If you want to relax the worry-tightened muscles in your face, let the half smile come to your face. As the half smile appears, all the facial muscles begin to relax. The longer the half smile is maintained, the better. It is the same smile you see on the face of the Buddha.

Place your left hand, palm side up, in your right palm. Let all the muscles in your hands, fingers, arms, and legs relax. Let go of everything. Be like the waterplants which flow with the current, while beneath the surface of the water the riverbed remains motionless. Hold on to nothing but your breath and the half smile.

For beginners, it is better to sit no longer than 20 or 30 minutes. During that time, you can readily obtain total rest. The technique for obtaining this rest lies in two things—watching and letting go: watching your breath, and letting go of everything else. Release every muscle in your body. After about 15 minutes or so, it is possible to reach a deep quiet filled with inner peace and joy. Maintain this quiet and peace.

Some people look on meditation as a toil and want the time to pass quickly in order to rest afterwards. Such persons do not know how to sit yet. If you sit correctly, it is possible to find total relaxation and peace right in the position of sitting. Often it helps to meditate on the image of a pebble thrown into a river.

How is one helped by the image of the pebble? Sit down in whatever position suits you best, the half lotus or lotus, back straight, the half smile on your face. Breathe slowly and deeply, following each breath, becoming one with the breath. Then let go of everything. Imagine yourself as a pebble which has been thrown into a river. The pebble sinks through the water effortlessly. Detached from everything, it falls by the shortest distance possible, finally reaching the bottom, the point of perfect rest. You are like a pebble which has let itself fall into the river, letting go of everything. At the center of your being is your breath. You don't need to know the length of time it takes before reaching the point of complete rest on the bed of fine sand beneath the water. When you feel yourself resting like a pebble which has reached the riverbed, that is the point when you begin to find your own rest. You are no longer pushed or pulled by anything.

If you cannot find joy in peace in these very moments of sitting, then the future itself will only flow by as a river flows by, you will not be able to hold it back, you will be incapable of living the future when it has become the present. Joy and peace are the joy and peace possible in this very hour of sitting. If you cannot find it here, you won't find it anywhere. Don't chase after your thoughts as a shadow follows its object. Don't run after your thoughts. Find joy and peace in this very moment.

This is your own time. This spot where you sit is your own spot. It is on this very spot and in this very moment that you can become enlightened. You don't have to sit beneath a special tree in a distant land. Practice like this for a few months, and you will begin to know a profound and renewing delight.

The ease of sitting depends on whether you practice mindfulness a little or a lot each day. And it depends on whether or not you sit regularly. Whenever possible, join with friends or relatives and organize an hour of sitting each night, say from 10 to 11. Whoever wishes could come to sit for a half hour, or even an entire hour.

Mindfulness of the mind

Someone might well ask: is relaxation then the only goal of meditation? In fact the goal of meditation goes much deeper than that. While relaxation is the necessary point of departure, once one has realized relaxation, it is possible to realize a tranquil heart and clear mind. To realize a tranquil heart and clear mind is to have gone far along the path of meditation.

Of course, to take hold of our minds and calm our thoughts, we must also practice mindfulness of our feelings and perceptions. To take hold of your mind, you must practice mindfulness of the mind. You must know how to observe and recognize the presence of every feeling and thought which arises in you. The Zen Master Thuong Chieu wrote, "If the practitioner knowns his own mind clearly he will obtain results with little effort. But if he does not know anything about his own mind, all of his effort will be wasted." If you want to know your own mind, there is only one way: to observe and recognize everything about it. This must be done at all times, during your day-to-day life no less than during the hour of meditation.

During meditation, various feelings and thoughts may arise. If you don't practice mindfulness of the breath, these thoughts will soon lure you away from mindfulness. But the breath isn't simply a means by which to chase away such thoughts and feelings. Breath remains the vehicle to unite body and mind and to open the gate to wisdom. When a feeling or thought arises, your intention should not be to chase it away, even if by continuing to concentrate on the breath the feeling or thought passes naturally from the mind. The intention isn't to chase it away, hate it, worry about it, or be frightened by it. So what exactly should you be doing concerning such thoughts and feelings? Simply acknowledge their presence. For example, when a feeling of sadness arises, immediately recognize it: "A feeling of sadness has just arisen in me." If the feeling of sadness continues, continue to recognize "A feeling of sadness is still in me." If there is a thought like, "It's late but the neighbors are surely making a lot of noise," recognize that the thought has arisen. If the thought continues to exist, continue to recognize it. If a different feeling or thought arises, recognize it in the same manner. The essential thing is not to let any feeling or thought arise without recognizing it in mindfulness, like a palace guard who is aware of every face that passes through the front corridor.

If there are no feelings or thoughts present, then recognize that there are no feelings or thoughts present. Practicing like this is to become mindful of your feelings and thoughts. You will soon arrive at taking hold of your mind. One can join the method of mindfulness of the breath with the mindfulness of feelings and thoughts.

The guard—or the monkey's shadow?

While practicing mindfulness, don't be dominated by the distinction between good and evil, thus creating a battle within oneself. Whenever a wholesome thought arises, acknowledge it: "A wholesome thought has just arisen." And if an unwholesome thought arises, acknowledge it as well: "An unwholesome thought has just arisen." Don't dwell on it or try to get rid of it, however much you don't like it. To acknowledge it is enough. If you have departed, then you must know that you have departed, and if you are still there, know that you are still there. Once you have reached such an awareness, there will be nothing you need fear anymore. When I mentioned the guard at the emperor's gate, perhaps you imagined a front corridor with two doors, one entrance and one exit, with your mind as the guard. Whatever feeling or thought enters, you are aware of its entrance, and when it leaves, you are aware of its exit. But the image has a shortcoming: it suggests that those who enter and exit the corridor are different from the guard. In fact our thoughts and feelings are us. They are a part of ourselves. There is a temptation to look upon them, or at least some of them, as an enemy force which is trying to disturb the concentration and understanding of your mind. But, in fact, when we are angry, *we ourselves* are anger. When we are happy, *we ourselves* are happiness. When we have certain thoughts, *we are those thoughts*. We are both the guard and the visitor at the same time. We are both the mind and the observer of the mind. Therefore, chasing away or dwelling on any thought isn't the important thing. The important thing is to be aware of the thought. This observation is not an objectification of the mind: it does not establish distinction between subject and object. Mind does not grab on to mind; mind does not push mind away. Mind can only observe itself. This observation isn't an observation of some object outside and independent of the observer.

Remember the Koan of the Zen Master Bach An who asked, "What is the sound of one hand clapping?" Or take the example of the taste the tongue experiences: what separates taste and tastebud? The mind experiences itself directly within itself. This is of special importance, and so in the Sutra of Mindfulness, Buddha always uses the phrasing "mindfulness of feeling in feeling, mindfulness of mind in mind." Some have said that the Buddha used this phrasing in order to put emphasis on such words as feeling and mind, but I don't think they have fully grasped the Buddha's intention. Mindfulness of feeling in feeling is mindfulness of feeling directly while experiencing feeling, and certainly not contemplation of some *image* of feeling which one creates to give feeling some objective, separate existence of its own outside of oneself. Descriptive words make it sound like a riddle or paradox or tongue twister: mindfulness of feeling in feeling is the mind experiencing mindfulness of the mind in the mind. The objectivity of an outside observer to examine something is the method of science, but it is not the method of meditation. Thus the image of the guard and the visitor fails to illustrate adequately the mindful observation of mind.

The mind is like a monkey swinging from branch to branch through a forest, says the Sutra. In order not to lose sight of the monkey by some sudden movement, we must watch the monkey constantly and even to be one with it. Mind contemplating mind is like an object and its shadow—the object cannot shake the shadow off. The two are one. Wherever the mind goes, it still lies in the harness of the mind. The Sutra sometimes uses the experession "Bind the monkey" to refer to taking hold of the mind. But the monkey image is only a means of expression. Once the mind is directly and continually aware of itself, it is no longer like a monkey. There are not two minds, one which swings from branch to branch and another which follows after to bind it with a piece of rope.

The person who practices meditation usually hopes to see into his or her own nature in order to obtain awakening. But if you are just beginning, don't wait to "see into your own nature." Better yet, don't wait for anything. Especially don't wait to see the Buddha or any

41

version of "ultimate reality" while you're sitting.

In the first six months, try only to build up your power of concentration, to create an inner calmness and serene joy. You will shake off anxiety, enjoy total rest, and quiet your mind. You will be refreshed and gain a broader, clearer view of things, and deepen and strengthen the love in yourself. And you will be able to respond more helpfully to all around you.

Sitting in meditation is nourishment for your spirit and nourishment for your body, as well. Through sitting, our bodies obtain harmony, feel lighter, and are more at peace. The path from the observation of your mind to seeing into your own nature won't be too rough. Once you are able to quiet your mind, once your feelings and thoughts no longer disturb you, at that point your mind will begin to dwell in mind. Your mind will take hold of mind in a direct and wondrous way which no longer differentiates between subject and object. Drinking a cup of tea, the seeming distinction between the one who drinks and the tea being drunk evaporates. Drinking a cup of tea becomes a direct and wondrous experience in which the distinction between subject and object no longer exists.

Dispersed mind is also mind, just as waves rippling in water are also water. When mind has taken hold of mind, deluded mind becomes true mind. True mind is our real self, is the Buddha: the pure one-ness which cannot be cut up by the illusory divisions of separate selves, created by concepts and language. But I don't want to say a lot about this.

Five ❀

One Is All, All Is One: The Five Aggregates

Let me devote a few lines here to talk about the methods you might use in order to arrive at liberation from narrow views, and to obtain fearlessness and great compassion. These are the contemplations on interdependence, impermanency, and compassion.

While you sit in meditation, after having taken hold of your mind, you can direct your concentration to contemplate on the interdependent nature of certain objects. This meditation is *not* a discursive reflection on a philosophy of interdependence. It is a penetration of mind into mind itself, using one's concentrative power to reveal the real nature of the object being contemplated.

Recall a simple and ancient truth: the subject of knowledge cannot exist independently from the object of knowledge. To see is to see something. To hear is to hear something. To be angry is to be angry over something. Hope is hope for something. Thinking is thinking about something. When the object of knowledge (the something) is not present, there can be no subject of knowledge. The practitioner meditates on mind and, by so doing, is able to see the interdependence of the subject of knowledge and the object of knowledge. When we practice mindfulness of breath, then the knowledge of breath is mind. When we practice mindfulness of the body, then the knowledge of body is mind. When we practice mindfulness of objects outside ourselves, then the knowledge of these objects is also mind. Therefore the contemplation of the nature of interdependence of all objects is also the contemplation of the mind.

Every object of the mind is itself mind. In Buddhism, we call the objects of mind the dharmas. Dharmas are usually grouped into five categories:

1. bodily and physical forms
2. feelings
3. perceptions
4. mental functionings
5. consciousness

These five categories are called *the five aggregates.* The fifth category, consciousness, however, contains all the other categories and is the basis of their existence.

Contemplation on interdependence is a deep looking into all dharmas in order to pierce through to their real nature, in order to see them as part of the great body of reality and in order to see that the great body of reality is indivisible. It cannot be cut into pieces with separate existences of their own.

The first object of contemplation is our own person, the assembly of the five aggregates in ourselves. You contemplate right here and now on the five aggregates which make up yourself.

You are conscious of the presence of bodily form, feeling, perception, mental functionings, and consciousness. You observe these "objects" until you see that each of them has intimate connection with the world outside yourself: if the world did not exist then the assembly of the five aggregates could not exist either.

Consider the example of a table. The table's existence is possible due to the existence of things which we might call "the non-table world": the forest where the wood grew and was cut, the carpenter, the iron ore which became the nails and screws, and countless other things which have relation to the table, the parents and ancestors of the carpenter, the sun and rain which made it possible for the trees to grow.

If you grasp the table's reality then you see that in the table itself are present all those things whch we normally think of as the non-table world. If you took away any of those non-table elements and returned them to their sources—the nails back to the iron ore, the wood to the forest, the carpenter to his parents—the table would no longer exist.

A person who looks at the table and can see the universe is a person who can see the way. You meditate on the assembly of the five aggregates in yourself in the same manner. You meditate on them until you are able to see the presence of the reality of one-ness in your own self, and can see that your own life and the life of the universe are one. If the five aggregates return to their sources, the self no longer exists. Each second, the world nourishes the five aggregates. The self is no different from the assembly of the five aggregates themselves. The assembly of the five aggregates plays, as well, a crucial role in the formation, creation, and destruction of all things in the universe.

Liberation from suffering

People normally cut reality into compartments, and so are unable to see the interdependence of all phenomena. To see one in all and all in one is to break through the great barrier which narrows one's perception of reality, a barrier which Buddhism calls the attachment to the false view of self.

Attachment to the false view of self means belief in the presence of unchanging entities which exist on their own. To break through this false view is to be liberated from every sort of fear, pain, and anxiety. When the Bodhisattva Quan the Am, who has been such a source of inspiration of peace workers in Vietnam, saw into the reality of the five aggregates giving rise to emptiness of Self, she was liberated from every suffering, pain, doubt, and anger. The same would apply to everyone. If we contemplate the five aggregates in a stubborn and diligent way, we, too, will be liberated from suffering, fear, and dread.

We have to strip away all the barriers in order to live as part of the universal life. A person isn't some private entity traveling unaffected through time and space as if sealed off from the rest of the world by a thick shell. Living for 100 or for 100,000 lives sealed off like that not only isn't living, but it isn't possible. In our lives are present a multitude of phenomena, just as we ourselves are present in many different phenomena. We are life, and life is limitless. Perhaps one can say that we are only alive when we live the life of the world, and so live the sufferings and joys of others. The suffering of others is our own suffering, and the happiness of others is our own happiness. If our lives have no limits, the assembly of the five aggregates which makes up our self also has no limits. The impermanent character of the universe, the successes and failures of life can no longer manipulate us. Having seen the reality of interdependence and entered deeply into its reality, nothing can oppress you any longer. You are liberated. Sit in the lotus position, observe your breath, and ask one who has died for others.

Meditation on interdependence is to be practiced constantly, not only while sitting, but as an integral part of our involvement in all ordinary tasks. We must learn to see that the person in front of us is ourself and that we are that person. We must be able to see the process of inter-origination and interdependence of all events, both those which are happening and those which will happen.

A ride on the waves of birth and death

I cannot leave out the problem of life and death. Many young people and others have come out to serve others and to labor for peace, through their love for all who are suffering. They are always mindful of the fact that the most important question is the question of life and death, but often not realizing that life and death are but two faces of one reality. Once we realize that we will have the courage to encounter both of them.

When I was only 19 years old, I was assigned by an older monk to meditate on the image of a corpse in the cemetery. But I found it very hard to take and resisted the meditation. Now I no longer feel that way. Then I thought that such a meditation should be reserved for older monks. But since then, I have seen many young soldiers lying motionless beside one another, some only 13, 14, and 15 years old. They had no preparation or readiness for death. Now I see that if one doesn't know how to die, one can hardly know how to live—because death is a part of life. Just two days ago Mobi told me that she thought at 20 one was old enough to meditate on the corpse. She has only turned 21 herself.

We must look death in the face, recognize and accept it, just as we look at and accept life.

The Buddhist Sutra on Mindfulness speaks about the meditation on the corpse: meditate on the decomposition of the body, how the body bloats and turns violet, how it is eaten by worms until only bits of blood and flesh still cling to the bones, meditate up to the point where only white bones remain, which in turn are slowly worn away and turn into dust. Meditate like that, knowing that your own body will undergo the same process. Meditate on the corpse until you are calm and at peace, until your mind and heart are light and tranquil and a smile appears on your face. Thus, by overcoming revulsion and fear, life will be seen as infinitely precious, every second of it worth living. And it is not just our own lives that are recognized as precious, but the lives of every other person, every other person, every other being, every other reality. We can no longer be deluded by the notion that the destruction of others' lives is necessary for our own survival. We see that life and death are but two faces of Life and that without both, Life is not possible, just as two sides of a coin are needed for the coin to exist. Only now is it possible to rise above birth and death, and to know how to live and how to die. The Sutra says that the Bodhisattvas who have seen into the reality of interdependence have broken through all narrow views, and have been able to enter birth and death as a person takes a ride in a small boat without being submerged or drowned by the waves of birth and death.

Some people have said that if you look at reality with the eyes of a Buddhist, you become pessimistic. But to think in terms of either pessimism or optimism oversimplifies the truth. The problem is to see reality as it is. A pessimistic attitude can never create the calm and serene smile which blossoms on the lips of the Bodhisattvas and all others who obtain the Way.

Six ❀

The Almond Tree
in Your Front Yard

I've spoken about the contemplation on interdependence. Of course all the methods in the search for truth should be looked on as means rather than as ends in themselves or as absolute truth. The meditation on interdependence is intended to remove the false barriers of discrimination so that one can enter into the universal harmony of life. It is not intended to produce a philosophical system, a philosophy of interdependence. Herman Hesse, in his novel *Siddartha*, did not yet see this and so his Siddhartha speaks about the philosophy of interdependence in words which strike us as somewhat naive. The author offers us a picture of interdependence in which everything is interrelated, a system in which no fault can be found: everything must fit into the foolproof system of mutual dependence, a system in which one cannot consider the problem of liberation in this world.

According to an insight of our tradition, reality has three natures: imagination, interdependence, and the nature of ultimate perfection. One first considers interdependence. Because of forgetfulness and prejudices, we generally cloak reality with a veil of false views and opinions. This is seeing reality through imagination. Imagination is an illusion of reality which conceives of reality as an assembly of small pieces of separate entities and selves. In order to break through, the practitioner meditates on the nature of interdependence or the interrelatedness of phenomena in the processes of creation and destruction. The consideration is a way of contemplation, not the basis of a philosophic doctrine. If one clings merely to a system of concepts, one only becomes stuck. The meditation on interdependence is to help one penetrate reality in order to be one with it, not to become caught up in philosophical opinion or meditation methods. The raft is used to cross the river. It isn't to be carried around on your shoulders. The finger which points at the moon isn't the moon itself.

Finally one proceeds to the nature of ultimate perfection—reality freed from all false views produced by the imagination. Reality is reality. It transcends every concept. There is no concept which can adequately describe it, not even the concept of interdependence. To assure that one doesn't become attached to a philosophical concept, our teaching speaks of the three *non*-natures to prevent the individual from becoming caught up in the doctrine of the three natures. The essence of Mahayana Buddhist teaching lies in this.

When reality is perceived in its nature of ultimate perfection, the practitioner has reached a level of wisdom called non-discrimination mind—a wondrous communion in which there is no longer any distinction made between subject and object. This isn't some far-off, unattainable state. Any one of us—by persisting in practicing even a little—can at least taste of it. I have a pile of orphan applications for sponsorship on my desk.* I translate a few each day. Before I begin to translate a sheet, I look into the eyes of the child in the photograph, and look at the child's expression and features closely. I feel a deep link between myself and each child, which allows me to enter a special communion with them. While writing this to you, I see that during those moments and hours, the communion I have experienced while translating the simple lines in the applications has been a kind of non-discrimination mind. I no longer see an "I" who translates the sheets to help each child, I no longer see a child who received love and help. The child and I are one: no one pities; no one asks for help; no one helps. There is no task, no social work to be done, no compassion, no special wisdom. These are moments of non-discrimination mind.

---

*The Vietnamese Buddhist Peace Delegation has carried on a program of raising financial support for families within Vietnam who took in orphans. In the United States the sponsor contributed $6 a month for the family of the orphan he or she was helping.

When reality is experienced in its nature of ultimate perfection, an almond tree that may be in your front yard reveals its nature in perfect wholeness. The almond tree is itself truth, reality, your own self. Of all the people who have passed by your yard, how many have really seen the almond tree? The heart of an artist may be more sensitive; hopefully he or she will be able to see the tree in a deeper way than many others. Because of a more open heart, a certain communion already exists between the artist and the tree. What counts is your own heart. If your heart is not clouded by false views, you will be able to enter into a natural communion with the tree. The almond tree will be ready to reveal itself to you in complete wholeness. To see the almond tree is to see the way. One Zen Master, when asked to explain the wonder of reality, pointed to a cypress tree and said, "Look at the cypress tree over there."

The voice of the rising tide

When your mind is liberated your heart floods with compassion: compassion for yourself, for having undergone countless sufferings because you were not yet able to relieve yourself of false views, hatred, ignorance, and anger; and compassion for others because they do not yet see and so are still imprisoned by false views, hatred, and ignorance and continue to create suffering for themselves and for others. Now you look at yourself and at others with the eyes of compassion, like a saint who hears the cry of every creature in the universe and whose voice is the voice of every person who has seen reality in perfect wholeness. As a Buddhist Sutra hears the voice of the Bodhisattva of compassion:

The wondrous voice, the voice of the one
    who attends to the cries of the world
The noble voice, the voice of the rising
    tide surpassing all the sounds of the
    world
Let our mind be attuned to that voice.

Put aside all doubt and meditate on the
    pure and holy nature of the regarder
    of the cries of the world
Because that is our reliance in situations
    of pain, distress, calamity, death.

Perfect in all merits, beholding all sentient
    beings with compassionate eyes, mak-
    ing the ocean of blessings limitless,
Before this one, we should incline.

Practice looking at all beings with the eyes of compassion: this is the meditation called "the meditation on compassion."

The meditation on compassion must be realized during the hours you sit and during every moment you carry out service for others. No matter where you go or where you sit, re-member the sacred call: "Look at all beings with the eyes of compassion."

There are many subjects and methods for

meditation, so many that I could never hope to write them all down for our friends. I've only mentioned a few, simple but basic methods here. A peace worker is like any one else. She or he must live her own life. Work is only a part of life. But work is life only when done in mindfulness. Otherwise, one becomes like the person "who lives as though dead." We need to light our own torch in order to carry on. But the life of each one of us is connected with the life of those around us. If we know how to live in mindfulness, if we know how to preserve and care for our own mind and heart, then thanks to that, our brothers and sisters will also know how to live in mindfulness.

Meditation reveals and heals

Sitting in mindfulness, both our bodies and minds can be at peace and totally relaxed. But this state of peace and relaxation differs fundamentally from the lazy, semi-conscious state of mind that one gets while resting and dozing. Sitting in such lazy semi-consciousness, far from being mindfulness, is like sitting in a dark cave. In mindfulness one is not only restful and happy, but alert and awake. Meditation is not evasion; it is a serene encounter with reality. The person who practices mindfulness should be no less awake than the driver of a car; if the practitioner isn't awake he will be possessed by dispersion and forgetfulness, just as the drowsy driver is likely to cause a grave accident. Be as awake as a person walking on high stilts—any

60

mis-step could cause the walker to fall. Be like a medieval knight walking weaponless in a forest of swords. Be like a lion, going forward with slow, gentle, and firm steps. Only with this kind of vigilance can you realize total awakening.

For beginners, I recommend the method of pure recognition: recognition without judgment. Feelings, whether of compassion or irritation, should be welcomed, recognized, and treated on an absolutely equal basis; because both are ourselves. The tangerine I am eating is me. The mustard greens I am planting are me. I plant with all my heart and mind. I clean this teapot with the kind of attention I would have were I giving the baby Buddha or Jesus a bath. Nothing should be treated more carefully than anything else. In mindfulness, compassion, irritation, mustard green plant, and teapot are all sacred.

When possessed by a sadness, an anxiety, a hatred, or a passion or whatever, the method of pure observation and recognition may seem difficult to practice. If so, turn to meditation on a fixed object, using your own state of mind as meditation's subject. Such meditation reveals and heals. The sadness or anxiety, hatred or passion, under the gaze of concentration and meditation reveals its own nature—a revelation that leads naturally to healing and emancipation. The sadness (or whatever has caused the pain) can be used as a means of liberation from torment and suffering, like using a thorn to remove a thorn. We should treat our anxiety,

our pain, our hatred and passion gently, respect-
fully, not resisting it, but living with it, making
peace with it, penetrating into its nature by
meditation on interdependence. One quickly
learns how to select subjects of meditation that
fit the situation. Subjects of meditation—like
interdependence, compassion, self, emptiness,
non-attachment—all these belong to the categories of meditation which have the power to
reveal and to heal.

Meditation on these subjects, however,
can only be successful if we have built up a
certain power of concentration, a power
achieved by the practice of mindfulness in
everyday life, in the observation and recognition of all that is going on. But the objects of
meditation must be realities that have real
roots in yourselves—not just subjects of philosophical speculation. Each should be like a kind
of food that must be cooked for a long time
over a hot fire. We put it in a pot, cover it, and
light the fire. The pot is ourselves and the heat
used to cook is the power of concentration.
The fuel comes from the continuous practice
of mindfulness. Without enough heat the food
will never be cooked. But once cooked, the
food reveals its true nature and helps lead us
to liberation.

The water clearer, the grass greener

The Buddha once said that the problem
of life and death is itself the problem of mindfulness. Whether or not one is alive depends

on whether one is mindful. In the Samyutta Nikaya Sutra, the Buddha tells a story which took place in a small village:

A famous dancer had just come to the village and the people were swarming the streets to catch a glimpse of her. At that same moment, a condemned criminal was obliged to cross the village carrying a bowl of oil filled to the very brim. He had to concentrate with all his might on keeping the bowl steady, for even if one drop of oil were to spill from the bowl to the ground, the soldier directly behind him had orders to take out his sword and cut off the man's head. Having reached this point in the story, Gautama Buddha asked: "Now, do you think our prisoner was able to keep all his attention so focused on the bowl of oil that his mind did not stray to steal a glimpse of the famous dancer in town, or to look up at the throngs of villagers making such a commotion in the streets, any of whom could bump into him at any moment?"

Another time the Buddha recounted a story which made me suddenly see the supreme importance of practicing mindfulness of one's own self—that is, to protect and care for one's self, not being preoccupied about the way others look after themselves, a habit of mind which gives rise to resentment and anxiety. The Buddha said, "There once were a couple of acrobats. The teacher was a poor widower and the student was a small girl named Meda. The two of them performed in the streets to earn enough to eat. They used a tall bamboo pole which the teacher balanced on the top of his head while the little girl slowly climbed to the top. There she remained while the teacher continued to walk along the ground.

"Both of them had to devote all their attention to maintain perfect balance and to prevent any accident from occurring. One day the teacher instructed the pupil: 'Listen, Meda, I will watch you and you watch me, so that we can help each other maintain concentration and balance and prevent an accident. Then we'll be sure to earn enough to eat.' But the little girl was wise and answered, 'Dear master, I think it would be better for each of us to watch ourself. To look after oneself means to look after both of us. That way I am sure we will avoid any accidents and will earn enough to eat.'" The Buddha said: "The child spoke correctly."

In a family, if there is one person who practices mindfulness, the entire family will be more mindful. Because of the presence of one member who lives in mindfulness, the entire family is reminded to live in mindfulness. If in one class, one student lives in mindfulness, the entire class is influenced.

In peace-serving communities, we must follow the same principle. Don't worry if those around you aren't doing their best. Just worry about how to make yourself worthy. Doing your best is the surest way to remind those around you to do their best. But to be worthy requires the continuing practice of mindfulness. That is a certainty. Only by practicing mindfulness will we not lose ourselves but acquire a bright joy and peace. Only by practicing mindfulness will we be able to look at everyone else with the open mind and eyes of love.

I was just invited downstairs for a cup of tea, into an apartment where a friend who helps us has a piano. As Kirsten—who is from Holland —poured tea for me, I looked at her pile of work and said, "Why don't you stop translating orphan applications for a minute and play the piano for me?" Kirsten was glad to put down her work for a moment and sat down at the piano to play a selection of Chopin she has known since she was a child. The piece has several measures which are soft and melodic but others which are loud and quick. Her dog was lying beneath the tea table, and when the music became excited, it began to bark and whine. I knew that it felt uneasy and wanted the music to stop. Kirsten's dog is treated with the kindness one gives to a small child, and perhaps is more sensitive to music than most children. Or perhaps it responded this way because its ears pick up certain vibrations that human ears do not. Kirsten continued to play while trying to console the dog at the same time, but to no avail. She finished and began to play another piece by Mozart which was light and harmonious. Now the dog lay quietly and appeared to be at peace. When Kirsten had finished she came over and sat down beside me and said, "Often when I play a piece of Chopin that is the least bit loud, the dog comes and grabs hold of my pantsleg, trying to force me to leave the piano. Sometimes I have to put her outside before I can continued playing. But whenever I play Bach or Mozart, she is peaceful."

Kirsten mentioned a report that in Canada people tried playing Mozart for their plants during the night. The plants grew more quickly than normal, and the flowers inclined toward the direction of the music. Others played Mozart every day in wheat and rye fields and were able to measure that the wheat and rye in these fields grew more quickly than the wheat and rye in other fields.

As Kirsten spoke, I thought about conference rooms where people argue and debate, where angry and reproachful words are hurled back and forth. If one placed flowers and plants in such rooms, chances are they would cease to grow.

I thought about the garden tended by a monk living in mindfulness. His flowers are always fresh and green, nourished by the peace and joy which flow from his mindfulness. One of the ancients said,

> When a great Master is born, the water in the rivers turns clearer and the plants grow greener.

We ought to listen to music or sit and practice breathing at the beginning of every meeting or discussion.

Seven ❀

Three Wondrous Answers

To end, let me retell a short story of Tolstoy's, the story of the Emperor's three questions. Tolstoy did not know the emperor's name . . .

One day it occurred to a certain emperor that if he only knew the answers to three questions, he would never stray in any matter.

What is the best time to do each thing?
Who are the most important people to work with?
What is the most important thing to do at all times?

The emperor issued a decree throughout his kingdom announcing that whoever could answer the questions would receive a great reward. Many who read the decree made their way to the palace at once, each person with a different answer.

In reply to the first question, one person

advised that the emperor make up a thorough time schedule, consecrating every hour, day, month, and year for certain tasks and then follow the schedule to the letter. Only then could he hope to do every task at the right time.

Another person replied that it was impossible to plan in advance and that the emperor should put all vain amusements aside and remain attentive to everything in order to know what to do at what time.

Someone else insisted that, by himself, the emperor could never hope to have all the foresight and competence necessary to decide when to do each and every task and what he really needed was to set up a Council of the Wise and then to act according to their advice.

Someone else said that certain matters required immediate decision and could not wait for consultation, but if he wanted to know in advance what was going to happen he should consult magicians and soothsayers.

The responses to the second question also lacked accord.

One person said that the emperor needed to place all his trust in administrators, another urged reliance on priests and monks, while others recommended physicians. Still others put their faith in warriors.

The third question drew a similar variety of answers.

Some said science was the most important pursuit. Others insisted on religion. Yet others claimed the most important thing was military skill.

The emperor was not pleased with any of the answers, and no reward was given.

After several nights of reflection, the emperor resolved to visit a hermit who lived up on the mountain and was said to be an enlightened man. The emperor wished to find the hermit to ask him the three questions, though he knew the hermit never left the mountains and was known to receive only the poor, refusing to have anything to do with persons of wealth or power. So the emperor disguised himself as a simple peasant and ordered his attendants to wait for him at the foot of the mountain while he climbed the slope alone to seek the hermit.

Reaching the holy man's dwelling place, the emperor found the hermit digging a garden in front of his hut. When the hermit saw the stranger, he nodded his head in greeting and continued to dig. The labor was obviously hard on him. He was an old man, and each time he thrust his spade into the ground to turn the earth, he heaved heavily.

The emperor approached him and said, "I have come here to ask your help with three questions: When is the best time to do each thing? Who are the most important people to work with? What is the most important thing to do at all times?"

The hermit listened attentively but only patted the emperor on the shoulder and continued digging. The emperor said, "You must be tired. Here, let me give you a hand with that." The hermit thanked him, handed the emperor the spade, and then sat down on the ground to rest.

After he had dug two rows, the emperor stopped and turned to the hermit and repeated his three questions. The hermit still did not answer, but instead stood up and pointed to the spade and said, "Why don't you rest now? I can take over again." But the emperor continued to dig. One hour passed, then two. Finally the sun began to set behind the mountain. The emperor put down the spade and said to the hermit, "I came here to ask if you could answer my three questions. But if you can't give me any answer, please let me know so that I can get on my way home."

The hermit lifted his head and asked the emperor, "Do you hear someone running over there?" The emperor turned his head. They both saw a man with a long white beard emerge from the woods. He ran wildly, pressing his hands against a bloody wound in his stomach. The man ran toward the emperor before falling unconscious to the ground, where he lay groaning. Opening the man's clothing, the emperor and hermit saw that the man had received a deep gash. The emperor cleaned the wound thoroughly and then used his own shirt to bandage it, but the blood completely soaked it within minutes. He rinsed the shirt out and bandaged the wound a second time and continued to do so until the flow of blood had stopped.

At last the wounded man regained consciousness and asked for a drink of water. The emperor ran down to the stream and brought back a jug of fresh water. Meanwhile, the sun had disappeared and the night air had begun to turn cold. The hermit gave the emperor a hand in carrying the man into the hut where they laid him down on the hermit's bed. The man closed his eyes and lay quietly. The emperor was worn out from a long day of climbing the mountain and digging the garden. Leaning against the doorway, he fell asleep. When he rose, the sun had already risen over the mountain. For a moment he forgot where he was and what he had come here for. He looked over to the bed and saw the wounded man also looking around him in confusion. When he saw the emperor, he stared at him intently and then said in a faint whisper, "Please forgive me."

"But what have you done that I should forgive you?" the emperor asked.

"You do not know me, your majesty, but I know you. I was your sworn enemy, and I had vowed to take vengeance on you, for during the last war you killed my brother and seized my property. When I learned that you were coming alone to the mountain to meet the hermit, I resolved to surprise you on your way back and kill you. But after waiting a long time there was still no sign of you, and so I left my ambush in order to seek you out. But instead of finding you, I came across your attendants, who recognized me, giving me this wound. Luckily, I escaped and ran here. If I hadn't met you I would surely be dead by now. I had intended to kill you, but instead you saved my life! I am ashamed and grateful beyond words. If I live, I vow to be your servant for the rest of my life, and I will bid my children and grandchildren to do the same. Please grant me your forgiveness."

The emperor was overjoyed to see that he was so easily reconciled with a former enemy. He not only forgave the man but promised to return all the man's property and to send his own physician and servants to wait on the man until he was completely healed. After ordering his attendants to take the man home, the emperor returned to see the hermit. Before returning to the palace the emperor wanted to repeat his three questions one last time. He found the hermit sowing seeds in the earth they had dug the day before.

The hermit stood up and looked at the emperor. "But your questions have already been answered."

"How's that?" the emperor asked, puzzled.

"Yesterday, if you had not taken pity on my age and given me a hand with digging these beds, you would have been attacked by that man on your way home. Then you would have deeply regretted not staying with me. Therefore the most important time was the time you were digging in the beds, the most important person was myself, and the most important pursuit was to help me. Later, when the wounded man ran up here, the most important time was the time you spent dressing his wound, for if you had not cared for him he would have died and you would have lost the chance to be reconciled with him. Likewise, he was the most important person, and the most important pursuit was taking care of his wound. Remember that there is only one important time and that is now. The present moment is the only time over which we have dominion. The most important person is always the person you are with, who is right before you, for who knows if you will have dealings with any other person in the future? The most important pursuit is making the person standing at your side happy, for that alone is the pursuit of life."

Tolstoy's story is like a story out of scripture: it doesn't fall short of any sacred text. We talk about social service, service to the people, service to humanity, service for others who are far away, helping to bring peace to the world—but often we forget that it is the very people around us that we must live for first of all. If you cannot serve your wife or husband or child or parent—how are you going to serve society? If you cannot make your own child happy, how do you expect to be able to make anyone else happy? If all our friends in the peace movement or of service communities of any kind do not love and help one another, whom can we love and help? Are we working for other humans, or are we just working for the name of an organization?

Service

The service of peace. The service of any person in need. The word service is so immense. Let's return first to a more modest scale: our families, our classmates, our friends, our own community. We must live for them—for if we cannot live for them, whom else do we think we are living for?

Tolstoy is a saint—what we Buddhists would call a Bodhisattva. But was the emperor himself able to see the meaning and direction of life? How can we live in the present moment, live right now with the people around us, helping to lessen their suffering and making their lives happier? How? The answer is this: We must practice mindfulness. The principle that Tolstoy gives appears easy. But if we want to put it into practice we must use the methods of mindfulness in order to seek and find the way.

I've written these pages for our friends to use. There are many people who have written about these things without having lived them, but I've only written down those things which I have lived and experienced myself. I hope you and your friends will find these things at least a little helpful along the path of our seeking: the path of our return.

❀ Exercises in Mindfulness

Here are a number of exercises and approaches in meditation which I often have used, adapting them from various methods to fit my own circumstances and preferences. Select the ones you like best and find the most suitable for your own self. The value of each method will vary according to each person's unique needs. Although these exercises are relatively easy, they form the foundations on which everything else is built.

Half-smile when you first wake up in the morning

Hang a branch, any other sign, or even the word "smile" on the ceiling or wall so that you see it right away when you open your eyes. This sign will serve as your reminder. Use these seconds before you get out of bed to take hold of your breath. Inhale and exhale three breaths gently while maintaining the half smile. Follow your breaths.

Half-smile during your free moments

Anywhere you find yourself sitting or standing, half-smile. Look at a child, a leaf, a painting on the wall, anything which is relatively still, and smile. Inhale and exhale quietly three times. Maintain the half smile and consider the spot of your attention as your own true nature.

Half-smile while listening to music

Listen to a piece of music for two or three minutes. Pay attention to the words, music, rhythm, and sentiments. Smile while watching your inhalations and exhalations.

Half-smile when irritated

When you realize you're irritated, half-smile at once. Inhale and exhale quietly, maintaining the half smile for three breaths.

Letting go in a lying-down position

Lie on your back on a flat surface without the support of mattress or pillow. Keep your two arms loosely by your sides and your two legs slightly apart, stretched out before you. Maintain a half smile. Breathe in and out gently, keeping your attention focused on your breath. Let go of every muscle in your body. Relax each muscle as though it were sinking down through the floor or as though it were as soft and yielding as a piece of silk hanging in the breeze to dry. Let go entirely, keeping your attention only on your breath and half smile. Think of yourself as a cat, completely relaxed before a warm fire, whose muscles yield without resistance to anyone's touch. Continue for 15 breaths.

Letting go in the sitting position

Sit in the half or full lotus, or cross-legged, or your two legs folded beneath you, or even on a chair, your two feet touching the floor. Half-smile. Inhale and exhale while maintaining the half smile. Let go.

Deep breathing

Lie on your back. Breathe evenly and gently, focusing your attention on the movement of your stomach. As you begin to breathe in, allow your stomach to rise in order to bring air into the lower half of your lungs. As the upper halves of your lungs begin to fill with air, your chest begins to rise and your stomach begins to lower. Don't tire yourself. Continue for 10 breaths. The exhalation will be longer than the inhalation.

Measuring your breath by your footsteps

Walk slowly and leisurely in a garden, along a river, or on a village path. Breathe normally. Determine the length of your breath, the exhalation and the inhalation, by the number of your footsteps. Continue for a few minutes. Begin to lengthen your exhalation by one step. Do not force a longer inhalation. Let it be natural. Watch your inhalation carefully to see if there is a desire to lengthen it. Continue for 10 breaths.

Now lengthen the exhalation by one more footstep. Watch to see whether the inhalation also lengthens by one step or not. Only lengthen the inhalation when you feel that it will give delight. After 20 breaths, return your breath to normal. About five minutes later, you can begin the practice of lengthened breaths again. When you feel the least bit tired, return to normal. After several sessions of the practice of lengthened breath, your exhalation and inhalation will grow equal in length. Do not practice long, equal breaths for more than 10 to 20 breaths before returning to normal.

Counting your breath

Sit in the half or full lotus or take a walk. As you inhale, be mindful that "I am inhaling, one." When you exhale, be mindful that "I am exhaling, one." Remember to breathe from the stomach. When beginning the second inhalation, be mindful that "I am inhaling, two." And slowly exhaling, be mindful that "I am exhaling, two." Continue on up through 10. After you have reached 10, return to one. Whenever you lose count, return to one.

Following your breath while listening to music

Listen to a piece of music. Breathe long, light, and even breaths. Follow your breath, be master of it while remaining aware of the movement and sentiments of the music. Do not get lost in the music, but continue to be master of your breath and your self.

Following your breath while carrying on a conversation

Breathe long, light, and even breaths. Follow your breath while listening to a friend's words and to your own replies. Continue as with the music.

Following the breath

Sit in a full or half lotus or go for a walk. Begin to inhale gently and normally (from the stomach), mindful that "I am inhaling normally." Exhale in mindfulness, "I am exhaling normally." Continue for three breaths. On the fourth breath, extend the inhalation, mindful that "I am breathing in a long inhalation." Exhale in mindfulness, "I am breathing out a long exhalation." Continue for three breaths.

Now follow your breath carefully, aware of every movement of your stomach and lungs. Follow the entrance and exit of air. Be mindful that "I am inhaling and following the inhalation from its beginning to its end. I am exhaling and following the exhalation from its beginning to its end."

Continue for 20 breaths. Return to normal. After 5 minutes, repeat the exercise. Remember to maintain the half smile while breathing. Once you have mastered this exercise, move on to the next.

Breathing to quiet the mind and body to realize joy

Sit in the full or half lotus. Half-smile. Follow your breath. When your mind and body are quiet, continue to inhale and exhale very lightly, mindful that, "I am breathing in and making the breath-body light and peaceful. I am exhaling and making the breath-body light and peaceful." Continue for three breaths, giving rise to the thought in mindfulness, "I am breathing in and making my entire body light and peaceful and joyous." Continue for three breaths and in mindfulness give rise to the thought, "I am breathing in while my body and mind are peace and joy. I am breathing out while my body and mind are peace and joy."

Maintain this thought in mindfulness from 5 to 30 minutes, or for an hour, according to your ability and to the time available to you. The beginning and end of the practice should be relaxed and gentle. When you want to stop, gently massage your eyes and face with your two hands and then massage the muscles in your legs before returning to a normal sitting position. Wait a moment before standing up.

Mindfulness of the positions of the body

This can be practiced in any time and place. Begin to focus your attention on your breath. Breathe quietly and more deeply than usual. Be mindful of the position of your body, whether you are walking, standing, lying, or sitting down. Know where you walk; where you stand; where you lie; where you sit. Be mindful of the purpose of your position. For example, you might be conscious that you are standing on a green hillside in order to refresh yourself, to practice breathing, or just to stand. If there is no purpose, be mindful that there is no purpose.

Mindfulness while making tea

Prepare a pot of tea to serve a guest or to drink by yourself. Do each movement slowly, in mindfulness. Do not let one detail of your movements go by without being mindful of it. Know that your hand lifts the pot by its handle. Know that you are pouring the fragrant warm tea into the cup. Follow each step in mindfulness. Breathe gently and more deeply than usual. Take hold of your breath if your mind strays.

Washing the dishes

Wash the dishes relaxingly, as though each bowl is an object of contemplation. Consider each bowl as sacred. Follow your breath to prevent your mind from straying. Do not try to hurry to get the job over with. Consider washing the dishes the most important thing in life. Washing the dishes is meditation. If you cannot wash the dishes in mindfulness, neither can you meditate while sitting in silence.

Washing clothes

Do not wash too many clothes at one time. Select only three or four articles of clothing. Find the most comfortable position to sit or stand so as to prevent a backache. Scrub the clothes relaxingly. Hold your attention on every movement of your hands and arms. Pay attention to the soap and water. When you have finished scrubbing and rinsing, your mind and body should feel as clean and fresh as your clothes. Remember to maintain the half smile and take hold of your breath whenever your mind wanders.

Cleaning house

Divide your work into stages: straightening things and putting away books, scrubbing the toilet, scrubbing the bathroom, sweeping the floors and dusting. Allow a good length of time for each task. Move slowly, three times more slowly than usual. Fully focus your attention on each task. For example, while placing a book on the shelf, look at the book, be aware of what book it is, know that you are in the process of placing it on the shelf, intending to put it in that specific place. Know that your hand reaches for the book, and picks it up. Avoid any abrupt or harsh movement. Maintain mindfulness of the breath, especially when your thoughts wander.

A slow-motion bath

Allow yourself 30 to 45 minutes to take a bath. Don't hurry for even one second. From the moment you prepare the bathwater to the moment you put on clean clothes, let every motion be light and slow. Be attentive of every movement. Place your attention to every part of your body, without discrimination or fear. Be mindful of each stream of water on your body. By the time you've finished, your mind should feel as peaceful and light as your body. Follow your breath. Think of yourself as being in a clean and fragrant lotus pond in the summer.

The pebble

While sitting still and breathing slowly, think of yourself as a pebble which is falling through a clear stream. While sinking, there is no intention to guide your movement. Sink toward the spot of total rest on the gentle sand of the river-bed. Continue meditating on the pebble until your mind and body are at complete rest: a pebble resting on the sand. Maintain this peace and joy a half hour while watching your breath. No thought about the past or future can pull you away from your present peace and joy. The universe exists in this present moment. No desire can pull you away from this present peace, not even the desire to become a Buddha or the desire to save all beings. Know that to become a Buddha and to save all beings can only be real-ized on the foundation of the pure peace of the present moment.

A day of mindfulness

Set aside one day of the week, any day that accords with your own situation. Forget the work you do during the other days. Do not organize any meetings or have friends over. Do only such simple work as house cleaning, cooking, washing clothes, and dusting.

Once the house is neat and clean, and all your things are in order, take a slow-motion bath. Afterwards, prepare and drink tea. You might read scripture or write letters to close friends. Afterwards, take a walk to practice breathing. While reading scripture or writing letters, maintain your mindfulness, don't let the text or letter pull you away to somewhere else. While reading the sacred text, know what you are reading; while writing the letter, know what you are writing. Follow the same procedure as listening to music or conversing with a friend. In the evening prepare yourself a light meal, perhaps only a little fruit or a glass of fruit juice. Sit in meditation for an hour before you go to bed. During the day, take two walks of a half hour to 45 minutes. Instead of reading before you go to bed, practice total relaxation for 5 to 10 minutes. Be master of your breathing. Breathe gently (the breath should not be too long), following the rising, the lowering of your stomach and chest, your eyes closed. Every movement during this day should be at least two times slower than usual.

Contemplation on interdependence

Find a photo of yourself as a child. Sit in the full or half lotus. Begin to follow your breath. After 20 breaths, begin to focus your attention on the photo in front of you. Recreate and live again the five aggregates of which you were made up at the time the photo was taken: the physical characteristics of your body, your feelings, perceptions, mind functionings, and consciousness at that age. Continue to follow your breath. Do not let your memories lure you away or overcome you. Maintain this meditation for 15 minutes. Maintain the half smile. Turn your mindfulness to your present self. Be conscious of your body, feelings, perceptions, mind functionings, and consciousness in the present moment. See the five aggregates which make up yourself. Ask the question, "Who am I?" The question should be deeply rooted in you, like a new seed nestled deep in the soft earth and damp with water. The question "Who am I?" should not be an abstract question to consider with your discursive intellect. The question "Who am I?" will not be confined to your intellect, but to the care of the whole of the five aggregates. Don't try to seek an intellectual answer. Contemplate for 10 minutes, maintaining light but deep breath to prevent being pulled away by philosophical reflection.

Yourself

Sit in a dark room by yourself, or alone by a river at night, or anywhere else where there is solitude. Begin to take hold of your breath. Give rise to the thought, "I will use my finger to point at myself," and then instead of pointing at your body, point away in the opposite direction. Contemplate seeing yourself outside of your bodily form. Contemplate seeing your bodily form present before you—in the trees, the grass and leaves, the river. Be mindful that you are in the universe and the universe is in you: if the universe is, you are; if you are, the universe is. There is no birth. There is no death. There is no coming. There is no going. Maintain the half smile. Take hold of your breath. Contemplate for 10 to 20 minutes.

Your skeleton

Lie on a bed, or on a mat or on the grass in a position in which you are comfortable. Don't use a pillow. Begin to take hold of your breath. Imagine all that is left of your body is a white skeleton lying on the face of the earth. Maintain the half smile and continue to follow your breath. Imagine that all your flesh has decomposed and is gone, that your skeleton is now lying in the earth 80 years after burial. See clearly the bones of your head, back, your ribs, your hip bones, leg and arm bones, finger bones. Maintain the half smile, breathe very lightly, your heart and mind serene. See that your skeleton is not you. Your bodily form is not you. Be at one with life. Live eternally in the trees and grass, in other people, in the birds and other beasts, in the sky, in the ocean waves. Your skeleton is only one part of you. You are present everywhere and in every moment. You are not only a bodily form, or even feelings, thoughts, actions, and knowledge. Continue for 20 to 30 minutes.

Your true visage before you were born

In the full or half lotus follow your breath. Concentrate on the point of your life's beginning—A. Know that it is also the point of beginning of your death. See that both your life and death are manifested at the same time: *this* is because *that* is, this could not have been if that were not. See that the existence of your life and death depend on each other: one is the foundation of the other. See that you are at the same time your life and your death; that the two are not enemies but two aspects of the same reality. Then concentrate on the point of ending of the twofold manifestation—B—which is wrongly called death. See that it is the ending point of the manifestation of both your life and your death.

See that there is no difference before A and after B. Search for your true face in the periods before A and after B.

A loved one who has died

On a chair or bed, sit or lie in a position you feel comfortable in. Begin to take hold of your breath. Contemplate the body of a loved one who has died, whether a few months or several years ago. Know clearly that all the flesh of the person has decomposed and only a skeleton remains lying quietly beneath the earth. Know clearly that your own flesh is still here and in yourself are still converged the five aggregates of bodily form, feeling, perception, mental functionings, and consciousness. Think of your interaction with that person in the past and right now. Maintain the half smile and take hold of your breath. Contemplate this way for 15 minutes.

Emptiness

Sit in the full or half lotus. Begin to regulate your breath. Contemplate the nature of emptiness in the assembly of the five aggregates: bodily form, feeling, perception, mind functionings, and consciousness. Pass from considering one aggregate to another. See that all transform, are impermanent and without self. The assembly of the five aggregates is like the assembly of all phenomena: all obey the law of interdependence. Their coming together and disbanding from one another resembles the gathering and vanishing of clouds around the peaks of mountains. Neither cling to nor reject the five aggregates. Know that like and dislike are phenomena which belong to the assemblage of the five aggregates. See clearly that the five aggregates are without self and are empty, but that they are also wondrous, wondrous as is each phenomenon in the universe, wondrous as the life which is present everywhere. Try to see that the five aggregates do not really undergo creation and destruction for they themselves are ultimate reality. Try to see by this contemplation that impermanence is a concept, nonself is a concept, emptiness is a concept, so that you will not become imprisoned in the concepts of impermanence, non-self, and emptiness. You will see that emptiness is also empty, and that the ultimate reality of emptiness is no different from the ultimate reality of the five aggregates. (*This exercise should* be practiced *only* after the student has thoroughly practiced the previous five exercises. The amount of time will be according to the individual—perhaps one hour, perhaps two.)

Compassion for the person you hate or despise the most

Sit quietly. Breathe and smile the half smile. Contemplate the image of the person who has caused you the most suffering. Regard the features you hate or despise the most or find the most repulsive. Try to examine what makes this person happy and what causes suffering in his daily life. Contemplate the person's perceptions; try to see what patterns of thought and reason this person follows. Examine what motivates this person's hopes and actions. Finally consider the person's consciousness. See whether his views and insights are open and free or not, and whether or not he has been influenced by any prejudices, narrow-mindedness, hatred, or anger. See whether or not he is master of himself. Continue until you feel compassion rise in your heart like a well filling with fresh water and your anger and resentment disappear. Practice this exercise many times on the same person.

Sit in the full or half lotus. Begin to follow your breath. Choose the situation of a person, family, or society which is suffering the most of any you know. This will be the object of your contemplation.

In the case of a person, try to see every suffering which that person is undergoing. Begin with the suffering of bodily form (sickness, poverty, physical pain) and then proceed to the suffering caused by feelings (internal conflicts, fear, hatred, jealousy, a tortured conscience). Consider next the suffering caused by perceptions (pessimism, dwelling on his problems with a dark and narrow viewpoint). See whether his mind functionings are motivated by fear, discouragement, despair, or hatred. See whether or not his consciousness is shut off because of his situation, because of his suffering, because of the people around him, his education, propaganda, or a lack of control of his own self. Meditate on all these sufferings until your heart fills with compassion like a well of fresh water, and you are able to see that the person suffers because of circumstances and ignorance. Resolve to help that person get out of his present situation through the most silent and unpretentious means possible.

In the case of a family, follow the same method. Go through all the sufferings of one person and then on to the next person until you have examined the sufferings of the entire family. See that their sufferings are your own. See that it is not possible to reproach even one person in that group. See that you must help them liberate themselves from their present situation by the most silent and unpretentious means possible.

In the case of a society, take the situation of a country suffering war or any other situation of injustice. Try to see that every person involved in the conflict is a victim. See that no person, including all those in warring parties or in what appear to be opposing sides, desires the suffering to continue. See that it is not only one or a few persons who are to blame for the situation. See that the situation is possible because of the clinging to ideologies and to an unjust world economic system which is upheld by every person through ignorance or through lack of resolve to change it. See that two sides in a conflict are not really opposing, but two aspects of the same reality. See that the most essential thing is life and that killing or oppressing one another will not solve anything. Remember the Sutra's words:

In the time of war
Raise in yourself the Mind of Compassion
Help living beings
Abandon the will to fight
Wherever there is furious battle
Use all your might
To keep both sides' strength equal
And then step into the conflict to reconcile

Vimalakirti Nirdesa

Meditate until every reproach and hatred disappears, and compassion and love rise like a well of fresh water within you. Vow to work for awareness and reconciliation by the most silent and unpretentious means possible.

Detached action

Sit in the full or half lotus. Follow your breath. Take a project in rural development or any other project which you consider important, as the subject of your contemplation. Examine the purpose of the work, the methods to be used, and the people involved. Consider first the purpose of the project. See that the work is to serve, to alleviate suffering, to respond to compassion, not to satisfy the desire for praise or recognition. See that the methods used encourage cooperation between humans. Don't consider the project as an act of charity. Consider the people involved. Do you still see in terms of ones who serve and ones who benefit? If you can still see who are the ones serving and who are the ones benefiting, your work is for the sake of yourself and the workers, and not for the sake of service. The Prajnaparamita Sutra says, "The Bodhisattva helps row living beings to the other shore but in fact no living beings are being helped to the other shore." Determine to work in the spirit of detached action.

Detachment

Sit in the full or half lotus. Follow your breath. Recall the most significant achievements in your life and examine each of them. Examine your talent, your virtue, your capacity, the convergence of favorable conditions that have led to success. Examine the complacency and the arrogance that have arisen from the feeling that you are the main cause for such success. Shed the light of interdependence on the whole matter to see that the achievement is not really yours but the convergence of various conditions beyond your reach. See to it that you will not be bound to these achievements. Only when you can relinquish them can you really be free and no longer assailed by them.

Recall the bitterest failures in your life and examine each of them. Examine your talent, your virtue, your capacity, and the absence of favorable conditions that led to the failures. Examine to see all the complexes that have arisen within you from the feeling that you are not capable of realizing success. Shed the light of interdependence on the whole matter to see that failures cannot be accounted for by your inabilities but rather by the lack of favorable conditions. See that you have no strength to shoulder these failures, that these failures are not your own self. See to it that you are free from them. Only when you can relinquish them can you really be free and no longer assailed by them.

Sit in the full or half lotus. Follow your breath. Apply one of the exercises on interdependence: yourself, your skeleton, or one who has died. See that everything is impermanent and without eternal identity. See that although things are impermanent and without lasting identity, they are nonetheless wondrous. While you are not bound by the conditioned, neither are you bound by the non-conditioned. See that the saint, though he is not caught by the teaching of interdependence, neither does he get away from the teaching. Although he can abandon the teaching as if it were cold ashes, still he can dwell in it and not be drowned. He is like a boat upon the water. Contemplate to see that awakened people, while not being enslaved by the work of serving living beings, never abandon their work of serving living beings.

Nhat Hanh: Seeing with the Eyes of Compassion

by James Forest

In 1968, I was traveling with Thich Nhat Hanh on a Fellowship [of Reconciliation] tour during which there were meetings with church and student groups, senators, journalists, professors, business people, and (blessed relief) a few poets. Almost everywhere he went, this brown-robed Buddhist monk from Vietnam (looking many years younger than the man in his forties he was) quickly disarmed those he met.

His gentleness, intelligence, and sanity made it impossible for most who encountered him to hang on to their stereotypes of what the Vietnamese were like. The vast treasury of the Vietnamese and Buddhist past spilled over through his stories and explanations. His interest in Christianity, even his enthusiasm for it, often inspired Christians to shed their condescension toward Nhat Hanh's tradition. He was able to help thousands of Americans glimpse the war through the eyes of peasants laboring in rice paddies and raising their children and grandchildren in villages surrounded by ancient groves of bamboo. He awoke the child within the adult as he described the craft of the village kite-maker and the sound of the wind instruments these fragile vessels would carry toward the clouds.

After an hour with him, one was haunted with the beauties of Vietnam, and filled with anguish at America's military intervention in the political and cultural tribulations of the Vietnamese people. One was stripped of all the ideological loyalties that justified one party or another in their battles, and felt the horror of the skies raked with bombers, houses and humans burned to ash, children left to face life without the presence and love of their parents and grandparents.

But there was one evening when Nhat Hanh awoke not understanding but rather the measureless rage of one American. He had been talking in the auditorium of a wealthy Christian church in a St. Louis suburb. As always, he emphasized the need for Americans to stop their bombing and killing in his country. There had been questions and answers when a large man stood up and spoke with searing scorn of the "supposed compassion" of "this Mr. Hanh."

"If you care so much about your people, Mr. Hanh, why are you here? If you care so much for the people who are wounded, why don't you spend your time with them?" At this point my recollection of his words is replaced by the memory of the intense anger which overwhelmed me.

When he finished, I looked toward Nhat Hanh in bewilderment. What could he—or anyone—say? The spirit of the war itself had suddenly filled the room, and it seemed hard to breathe.

There was a silence. Then Nhat Hanh began to speak—quietly, with deep calm, indeed with a sense of personal caring for the man who had just damned him. The words seemed like rain falling on fire. "If you want the tree to grow," he said, "it won't help to water the leaves. You have to water the roots. Many of the roots of the war are here, in your country. To help the people who are to be bombed, to try to protect them from this suffering, I have to come here."

The atmosphere in the room was transformed. In the man's fury we had experienced our own furies; we had seen the world as through a bomb bay. In Nhat Hanh's response we had experienced an alternate possibility: the possibility (here brought to Christians by a Buddhist and to Americans by an "enemy") of overcoming hatred with love, of breaking the seemingly endless chain reaction of violence throughout human history.

But after his response, Nhat Hanh whispered something to the chairman and walked quickly from the room. Sensing something was wrong, I followed him out. It was a cool, clear night. Nhat Hanh stood on the sidewalk beside the church parking lot. He was struggling for air—like someone who had been deeply under-water and who had barely managed to swim to the surface before gasping for breath. It was several minutes before I dared ask him how he was or what had happened.

Nhat Hanh explained that the man's com-ments had been terribly upsetting. He had wanted to respond to him with anger. So he had made himself breathe deeply and very slowly in order to find a way to respond with calm and understanding. But the breathing had been too slow and too deep.

"Why not be angry with him," I asked. "Even pacifists have a right to be angry."

"If it were just myself, yes. But I am here to speak for Vietnamese peasants. I have to show them what we can be at our best."

The moment was an important one in my life, one pondered again and again since then. For one thing, it was the first time that I real-ized there was a connection between the way one breathes and the way one responds to the world around.

Until very recently, Nhat Hanh has made no attempt to teach Western people any of the skills of meditation—what he often calls mind-fulness. Only during the past year, first with a few Western friends helping the Vietnamese Buddhist Peace Delegation in Paris, later with a group at that city's Quaker International Center, has he begun to teach meditation. Now he has written a small book on the subject, *The Miracle of Mindfulness*, a manual on meditation.

Nhat Hanh is a poet, Zen Master, and a co-chairman of the Fellowship of Reconciliation. In Vietnam, he played a major role in the creation of "engaged Buddhism"—a profound religious renewal rooted in compassion and service out of which emerged countless projects which combined help to the war's victims with nonviolent opposition to the war itself. For their work, thousands of Buddhists—nuns, monks, and lay people—were shot or imprisoned.

His work in Vietnam gave birth to the School of Youth for Social Service, Van Hanh University, a small monastery that was an early base of the nonviolent movement, a pacifist underground press (led by his co-worker Cao Ngoc Phuong), and the La Boi Press, one of the principal vehicles of cultural and religious renewal.

His poetry provides the words of many of the most popular songs in contemporary Vietnam, songs of hope surviving grief.

Even in exile, representing overseas the Unified Buddhist Church of Vietnam, he has continued to be a force for nonviolence and reconciliation in his homeland and an organizer of supportive responses from other countries. (His friendship with Martin Luther King was a factor in Dr. King's decision to ignore the advice of many colleagues and contributors who opposed his "mixing issues" and to join in the opposition to the Vietnam war. Shortly before his assassination, Dr. King nominated Nhat Hanh for the Nobel Prize for Peace.)

Only a few of his books have been published outside of Vietnam: *Lotus in a Sea of Fire*, *The Cry of Vietnam*, *The Path of Return Continues the Journey*, *Zen Keys*, and *The Raft Is Not the Shore*.

During conversations with Nhat Hanh and his co-workers in Paris, in the apartment of the Vietnamese Buddhist Peace Delegation, our thoughts turned to the absence of a meditative dimension in much of the American peace movement. Its absence helped explain why so much of the "peace" movement (perhaps better called the American-withdrawal movement) had exhibited such slight and superficial interest in the Buddhists' nonviolent campaign against the war. The weaponless Buddhists were not judged truly "political," merely a religious movement: admirable, unusually courageous when compared to other religious groups, but peripheral.

What American peace activists might learn from their Vietnamese counterparts is that, until there is a more meditative dimension in the peace movement, our perceptions of reality (and thus our ability to help occasion understanding and transformation) will be terribly crippled. Whatever our religious or nonreligious background and vocabulary may be, we will be overlooking something as essential to our lives and work as breath itself.

Breath itself. Breathing. It comes to many as astonishing news that something as simple as attention to breathing has a central part to play in meditation and prayer. It is like a mystery novelist's idea of hiding the diamonds in the goldfish bowl: too obvious to notice. But since the news has made its way past my own barriers of skepticism, there has been no end of confirmations—principally, the confirmation of experience.

The problem with meditation is that the contexts for it are too close at hand. The chances, as Nhat Hanh points out, are scattered everywhere: in the bathtub, in the kitchen sink, on a cutting board, a sidewalk or path, on a tenement staircase, on a picket line, at a typewriter . . . literally anywhere. The moments and places of silence and stillness are wondrous and helpful, but not indispensable. The meditative life doesn't require a secluded, greenhouse existence. (It does need occasional periods of time, even a whole day of the week, when special attention can be given to becoming more mindful. But then Christians and Jews ought not to be newcomers to the Sabbath.)

To the skeptic, Nhat Hanh's suggestions will seem quite absurd, a bad joke at the end of history, the latest card trick dealt out of the ancient deck of mystical doubletalk. But the pacifist affirmation itself strikes many as no smaller an absurdity: choosing to nurture life and to live without weapons in a murderous world. The way of meditation only carries that personal disarmament we have already begun an essential step deeper—nonviolence not only in the face of governments and corporations and liberation armies but a nonviolent encounter with reality itself.

This is the way to understand a simple truth

Nhat Hanh has mentioned elsewhere: "Those who are without compassion cannot see what is seen with the eyes of compassion." That more inclusive sight makes the small but crucial difference between despair and hope.

❁

Selection of
Buddhist Sutras

❀ The Foundation of Mindfulness

(Satipaṭṭhāna Sutta)

Translated from the Pali by Nyānasatta

Thus have I heard. At one time the Blessed One was living among the Kurus, at Kammasadamma—a market town of the Kuru people. There the Blessed One addressed the bhikkhus thus: "Monks," and they replied to him, "Venerable Sir." The Blessed One spoke as follows:

This is the only way, monks, for the purification of beings, for the overcoming of sorrow and lamentation, for the destruction of suffering and grief, for reaching the right path, for the attainment of Nirvāna, namely the four Foundations of Mindfulness. What are the four?

Herein (in this teaching) a monk lives contemplating the body in the body, ardent, clearly comprehending and mindful, having overcome, in this world, covetousness and grief; he lives contemplating feelings in feelings, ardent, clearly comprehending and mindful, having overcome, in this world, covetousness and grief; he lives contemplating consciousness in consciousness, ardent, clearly comprehending and mindful, having overcome, in this world, covetousness and grief; he lives contemplating mental objects in mental objects, ardent, clearly comprehending and mindful, having overcome, in this world, covetousness and grief.

I. The Contemplation of the Body

1. *Mindfulness of Breathing*

And how does a monk live contemplating the body in the body?

Herein, monks, a monk having gone to the forest, to the foot of a tree or to an empty place, sits down, with his legs crossed, keeps his body erect and his mindfulness alert.

Ever mindful he breathes in, and mindful he breathes out. Breathing in a long breath, he knows "I am breathing in a long breath"; breathing out a long breath, he knows "I am breathing out a long breath"; breathing in a short breath, he knows "I am breathing in a short breath"; breathing out a short breath, he knows "I am breathing out a short breath."

"Experiencing the whole (breath-) body, I shall breathe in," thus he trains himself. "Experiencing the whole (breath-) body, I shall breathe out," thus he trains himself. "Calming the activity of the (breath-) body, I shall breathe in," thus he trains himself. "Calming the activity of the (breath-) body, I shall breathe out," thus he trains himself.

Just as a skillful turner or turner's apprentice, making a long turn, knows "I am making a long turn," or making a short turn, knows, "I am making a short turn," just so the monk, breathing in a long breath, knows "I am breathing in a long breath"; breathing out a long breath, knows "I am breathing out a long breath"; breathing in a short breath, knows "I am breathing in a short breath"; breathing out a short breath, knows "I am breathing out a short breath." "Experiencing the whole (breath-) body, I shall breathe in," thus he trains himself. "Experiencing the whole (breath-) body, I shall breathe out," thus he trains himself. "Calming the activity of the (breath-) body, I shall breathe in," thus he trains himself. "Calming the activity of the (breath-) body, I shall breathe out," thus he trains himself.

Thus he lives contemplating the body in the body internally, or he lives contemplating the body in the body, internally and externally. He lives contemplating origination-factors in the body, or he lives contemplating origination-and-dissolution factors in the body. Or his mindfulness is established with the thought: "The body exists," to the extent necessary just for knowledge and mindfulness, and he lives detached, and clings to naught in the world. Thus also, monks, a monk lives contemplating the body in the body.

2. The Postures of the Body

And further, monks, a monk knows when he is going "I am going"; he knows when he is standing "I am standing"; he knows when he is sitting "I am sitting"; he knows when he is lying down "I am lying down"; or just as his body is disposed so he knows it.

Thus he lives contemplating the body in the body internally, or he lives contemplating the body in the body externally, or he lives contemplating the body in the body internally and externally. He lives contemplating origination-factors in the body, or he lives contemplating origination-and-dissolution factors in the body. Or his mindfulness is established with the thought: "The body exists," to the extent necessary just for knowledge and mindfulness, and he lives detached, and clings to naught in the world. Thus also, monks, a monk lives contemplating the body in the body.

3. Mindfulness with Clear Comprehension

And further, monks, a monk, in going forward and back, applies clear comprehension; in looking away, he applies clear comprehension; in bending and in stretching, he applies clear comprehension; in wearing robes and carrying the bowl, he applies clear comprehension; in eating, drinking, chewing, and savoring, he applies clear comprehension; in attending to the calls of nature, he applies clear comprehension; in walking, standing, in sitting, in falling asleep, in waking, in speaking and in keeping silence, he applies clear comprehension.

Thus he lives contemplating the body in the body . . .

4. The Reflection on the Repulsiveness of the Body

And further, monks, a monk reflects on this very body enveloped by the skin and full of manifold impurity, from the soles up, and from the top of the head-hair down, thinking thus: "There are in this body hair of the head, hair of the body, nails, teeth, skin, flesh, sinews, bones, marrow, kidneys, heart, liver, midriff,

114

spleen, lungs, intestines, mesentery, gorge, feces, bile, phlegm, pus, blood, sweat, fat, tears, grease, saliva, nasal mucus, synovial fluid, urine."

Just as if there were a double-mouthed provision bag full of various kinds of grain such as hill paddy, paddy, green gram, cow-peas, sesame, and husked rice, and a man with sound eyes, having opened that bag, were to take stock of the contents thus: This is hill paddy, this is paddy, this is green gram, this is cow-pea, this is sesame, this is husked rice. Just so, monks, a monk reflects on this very body enveloped by the skin and full of manifold impurity, from the soles up, and from the top of the head-hair down, thinking thus: "There are in this body hair of the head, hair of the body, nails, teeth, skin, flesh, sinews, bones, marrow, kidneys, heart, liver, midriff, spleen, lungs, intestines, mesentery, gorge, feces, bile, phlegm, pus, blood, sweat, fat, tears, grease, saliva, nasal mucus, synovial fluid, urine."

Thus he lives contemplating the body in the body . . .

5. The Reflection on the Material Elements

And further, monks, a monk reflects on this very body, however it be placed or disposed, by way of the material elements: "There are in this body the element of earth, the element of water, the element of fire, the element of wind."

Just as if, monks, a clever cow-butcher or his apprentice, having slaughtered a cow and divided it into portions, should be sitting at the junction of four high roads, in the same way, a monk reflects on this very body, as it is placed or disposed, by way of the material elements: "There are in this body the elements of earth, water, fire, and wind."

Thus he lives contemplating the body in the body . . .

6. The Nine Cemetery Contemplations

And further, monks, as if a monk sees a body dead one, two, or three days; swollen, blue, and festering, thrown in the charnel ground, he then applies this perception to his own body thus: "Verily, also my own body is of the same nature; such it will become and will not escape it."

Thus he lives contemplating the body in the body internally, or lives contemplating the body in the body externally, or lives contemplating the body in the body internally and externally. He lives contemplating origination-factors in the body, or he lives contemplating dissolution-factors in the body, or he lives contemplating origination-and-dissolution-factors in the body. Or his mindfulness is established with the thought: "The body exists," to the extent necessary just for knowledge and mindfulness, and he lives independent, and clings to naught in the world. Thus also, monks, a monk lives contemplating the body in the body.

2. And further, monks, as if a monk sees a body thrown in the charnel ground, being eaten by crows, hawks, vultures, dogs, jackals, or by different kinds of worms, he then applies this perception to his own body thus: "Verily, also my own body is of the same nature; such it will become and will not escape it."

Thus he lives contemplating the body in the body . . .

3. And further, monks, as if a monk sees a body thrown in the charnel ground and reduced to a skeleton with some flesh and blood attached to it, held together by the tendons . . .

4. And further, monks, as if a monk sees a body thrown in the charnel ground, and reduced to a skeleton, blood-besmeared and 'without flesh, held together by the tendons . . .

5. And further, monks, as if a monk sees a body thrown in the charnel ground and reduced to a skeleton without flesh and blood, held together by the tendons . . .

6. And further, monks, as if a monk sees a body thrown in the charnel ground and reduced to disconnected bones, scattered in all directions—here a bone of the hand, there a bone of the foot, a shin bone, a thigh bone, the pelvis, spine and skull . . .

7. And further, monks, as if a monk sees a body thrown in the charnel ground, reduced to bleached bones of conch-like color . . .

8. And further, monks, as if a monk sees a body thrown in the charnel ground, reduced to bones, more than a year old, lying in a heap . . .

9. And further, monks, as if a monk sees a body thrown in the charnel ground, reduced to bones, gone rotten and become dust, he then applies this perception to his own body thus: "Verily, also my own body is of the same nature; such it will become and will not escape it."

Thus he lives contemplating the body in the body internally, or he lives contemplating the body in the body externally, or he lives contemplating the body in the body internally and externally. He lives contemplating origination-factors in the body, or he lives contemplating dissolution-factors in the body, or he lives contemplating origination-and-dissolution-factors in the body. Or his mindfulness is established with the thought: "The body exists," to the extent necessary just for knowledge and mindfulness, and he lives detached, and clings to naught in the world. Thus also, monks, a monk lives contemplating the body in the body.

II. The Contemplation of Feeling

And how, monks, does a monk live contemplating feelings in feelings?

Herein, monks, a monk when experiencing a pleasant feeling knows, "I experience a pleasant feeling"; when experiencing a painful feeling, he knows, "I experience a painful feeling"; when experiencing a neither pleasant nor painful feeling, he knows, "I experience a neither pleasant nor painful feeling"; when experiencing a pleasant worldly feeling, he knows, "I experience a pleasant worldly feeling"; when experiencing a pleasant spiritual feeling, he knows, "I experience a pleasant spiritual feeling"; when experiencing a painful worldly feeling, he knows, "I experience a painful worldly feeling"; when experiencing a painful spiritual feeling, he knows, "I experience a painful spiritual feeling"; when experiencing a neither pleasant nor painful worldly feeling, he knows, "I experience a neither pleasant nor painful worldly feeling"; when experiencing a neither pleasant nor painful spiritual feeling, he knows, "I experience a neither pleasant nor painful spiritual feeling."

Thus he lives contemplating feelings in feelings internally, or he lives contemplating feelings in feelings externally, or he lives contemplating feelings in feelings internally and externally. He lives contemplating origination-factors in feelings, or he lives contemplating dissolution-factors in feelings, or he lives contemplating origination-and-dissolution factors in feelings. Or his mindfulness is established with the thought, "Feeling exists," to the extent necessary just for knowledge and mindfulness, and he lives detached, and clings to naught in the world. Thus, monks, a monk lives contemplating feelings in feelings.

III. The Contemplation of Consciousness

And how, monks, does a monk live contemplating consciousness in consciousness?

Herein, monks, a monk knows the consciousness with lust, as with lust; the consciousness without lust, as without lust; the consciousness with hate, as with hate; the consciousness without hate, as without hate; the consciousness with ignorance, as with ignorance; the consciousness without ignorance, as without ignorance; the shrunken state of consciousness as the shrunken state; the distracted state of consciousness as the distracted state; the developed state of consciousness as the developed state; the undeveloped state of consciousness as the undeveloped state; the state of consciousness with some other mental state superior to it, as the state with something mentally higher; the state of consciousness with no other mental state superior to it, as the state with nothing mentally higher;

119

the concentrated state of consciousness as the concentrated state; the unconcentrated state of consciousness as the unconcentrated state; the freed state of consciousness as the freed state; and the unfreed state of unconsciousness as the unfreed.

Thus he lives contemplating consciousness in consciousness internally or he lives contemplating consciousness in consciousness externally, or he lives contemplating consciousness in consciousness internally and externally. He lives contemplating origination-factors in consciousness, or he lives contemplating dissolution-factors in consciousness, or he lives contemplating origination-and-dissolution-factors in conousness. Or his mindfulness is established with the thought, "Consciousness exists," to the extent necessary just for knowledge and mindfulness, and he lives detached and clings to naught in the world. Thus, monks, a monk lives contemplating consciousness in consciousness.

IV. The Contemplation of Mental Objects

1. The Five Hindrances

And how, monks, does a monk live contemplating mental objects in mental objects?

Herein, monks, a monk lives contemplating mental objects in the mental objects of the five hindrances.

How, monks, does a monk live contemplating mental objects in the mental objects of the five hindrances?

Herein, monks, a monk, when sense-desire is present, knows, "There is sense-desire in me," or when sense-desire is not present, he knows, "There is no sense desire in me." He knows how the arising of the nonarisen sense-desire comes to be; he knows how the abandoning of the arisen sense-desire comes to be; and he knows how the nonarising in the future of the abandoned sense-desire comes to be.

When anger is present, he knows, "There is anger in me," or when anger is not present, he knows, "There is no anger in me." He knows how the arising of the nonarisen anger comes to be; he knows how the abandoning of the arisen anger comes to be; and he knows how the nonarising in the future of the abandoned anger comes to be.

When sloth and torpor are present, he knows, "There are sloth and torpor in me," and when sloth and torpor are not present, he knows, "There are no sloth and torpor in me." He knows how the arising of the nonarisen sloth and torpor comes to be; he knows how the abandoning of the arisen sloth and torpor comes to be; and he knows how the nonarising in the future of the abandoned sloth and torpor comes to be.

When agitation and scruples are present, he knows, "There are agitation and scruples in me," or when agitation and scruples are not present, he knows, "There are no agitation and scruples in me." He knows how the arising of the nonarisen agitation and scruples comes to be; he knows how the abandoning of the arisen agitation and scruples comes to be; and he knows how the nonarising in the future of the abandoned agitation and scruples comes to be.

When doubt is present, he knows, "There is doubt in me," or when doubt is not present, he knows, "There is no doubt in me." He knows how the arising of the nonarisen doubt comes to be; he knows how the

121

abandoning of the arisen doubt comes to be; he knows how the nonarising in the future of the abandoned doubt comes to be.

Thus he lives contemplating mental objects in mental objects internally, or he lives contemplating mental objects in mental objects externally, or he lives contemplating mental objects in mental objects internally and externally. He lives contemplating origination-factors in mental objects, or he lives contemplating dissolution-factors in mental objects, or he lives contemplating origination-and-dissolution-factors in mental objects. Or his mindfulness is established with the thought, "Mental objects exist," to the extent necessary just for knowledge and mindfulness, and he lives detached, and clings to naught in the world. Thus also, monks, a monk lives contemplating mental objects in the mental objects of the five hindrances.

2. The Five Aggregates of Clinging

And further, monks, a monk lives contemplating mental objects in the mental objects of the five aggregates of clinging.

How, monks, does a monk live contemplating mental objects in the mental objects of the five aggregates of clinging?

Herein, monks, a monk thinks, "Thus is material form; thus is the arising of material form; and thus is the disappearance of material form. Thus is feeling; thus is the arising of feeling; thus is the disappearance of feeling. Thus is perception; thus is the arising of perception; thus is the disappearance of perception. Thus are formations; thus is the arising of formations; and thus is the disappearance of formations. Thus is consciousness; thus is the arising of consciousness; and thus is the disappearance of consciousness."

Thus he lives contemplating mental objects in mental objects internally, or he lives contemplating mental objects in mental objects externally, or he lives contemplating mental objects in mental objects internally and externally. He lives contemplating origination-factors in mental objects, or he lives contemplating dissolution-factors in mental objects, or he lives contemplating origination-and-dissolution-factors in mental objects. Or his mindfulness is established with the thought, "Mental objects exist," to the extent necessary just for knowledge and mindfulness, and he lives detached, and clings to naught in the world. Thus also, monks, a monk lives contemplating mental objects in the mental objects of the five aggregates of clinging.

3. The Six Internal and the Six External Sense-Bases

And further, monks, a monk lives contemplating mental objects in the mental objects of the six internal and the six external sense-bases.

How, monks, does a monk live contemplating mental objects in the mental objects of the six internal and the six external sense-bases?

Herein, monks, a monk knows the eye and visual forms, and the fetter that arises dependent on both (the eye and forms); he knows how the arising of the nonarisen fetter comes to be; he knows how the abandoning of the arisen fetter comes to be; and he knows how the nonarising in the future of the abandoned fetter comes to be.

He knows the ear and sounds . . . the nose and smells . . . the tongue and flavors . . . the body and tactile objects . . . the mind and mental objects, and the fetter that arises dependent on both; he knows how the abandoning of the nonarisen fetter comes to be; and he knows how the nonarising in the future of the abandoned fetter comes to be.

Thus, monks, the monk lives contemplating mental objects in mental objects internally, or he lives contemplating mental objects in mental objects externally, or he lives contemplating mental objects in mental objects internally and externally. He lives contemplating origination-factors in mental objects, or he lives contemplating dissolution-factors in mental objects, or he lives contemplating origination-and-dissolution-factors in mental objects. Or his mindfulness is established with the thought, "Mental objects exist," to the extent necessary just for knowledge and mindfulness, and he lives detached, and clings to naught in the world. Thus, monks, a monk lives contemplating mental objects in the mental objects of the six internal and the six external sense-bases.

4. The Seven Factors of Enlightenment

And further, monks, a monk lives contemplating mental objects in the mental objects of the seven factors of enlightenment.

How, monks, does a monk live contemplating mental objects in the mental objects of the seven factors of enlightenment?

Herein, monks, when the enlightenment-factor of mindfulness is present the monk knows, "The enlightenment-factor of mindfulness is in me," or when the enlightenment-factor of mindfulness is absent, he knows, "The enlightenment-factor of mindfulness is not in me"; and he knows how the arising of the nonarisen enlightenment-factor of mindfulness comes to be; and how perfection in the development of the arisen enlightenment-factor of mindfulness comes to be.

When the enlightenment-factor of the investigation of mental objects is present, the monk knows, "The enlightenment-factor of the investigation of mental objects is in me"; when the enlightenment-factor of the investigation of mental objects is absent, he knows, "The enlightenment-factor of the investigation of mental objects is not in me"; and he knows how the arising of the nonarisen enlightenment-factor of the investigation of mental objects comes to be, and how perfection in the development of the arisen enlightenment-factor of the investigation of mental objects comes to be.

When the enlightenment-factor of energy is present, he knows, "The enlightenment-factor of energy is in me"; when the enlightenment-factor of energy is absent, he knows, "The enlightenment-factor of energy is not in me"; and he knows how the arising of the nonarisen enlightenment-factor of energy comes to be, and how perfection in the development of the arisen enlightenment-factor of energy comes to be.

When the enlightenment-factor of joy is present, he knows, "The enlightenment-factor of joy is in me"; and when the enlightenment-factor of joy is absent, he knows, "The enlightenment-factor of joy is not in me"; and he knows how the arising of the nonarisen enlightenment-factor of joy comes to be, and how perfection in the development of the arisen enlightenment-factor of joy comes to be.

When the enlightenment-factor of tranquility is present, he knows, "The enlightenment-factor of tranquility is in me"; when the enlightenment-factor of tranquility is absent, he knows, "The enlightenment-factor of tranquility is not in me"; and he knows how the arising of the nonarisen enlightenment-factor of tranquility comes to be, and how perfection in the development of the arisen enlightenment-factor of tranquility comes to be.

When the enlightenment-factor of concentration is present, he knows, "The enlightenment-factor of concentration is in me"; when the enlightenment-factor of concentration is absent, he knows, "The enlightenment-factor of concentration is not in me"; and he knows how the arising of the nonarisen enlightenment-factor of concentration comes to be, and how perfection in the development of the arisen enlightenment-factor of concentration comes to be.

When the enlightenment-factor of equanimity is present, he knows, "The enlightenment-factor of equanimity is in me"; when the enlightenment factor of equanimity is absent, he knows, "The enlightenment-factor of equanimity is not in me"; and he knows how the arising of the nonarisen enlightenment-factor of equanimity comes to be, and how perfection in the development of the arisen enlightment-factor of equanimity comes to be.

Thus he lives contemplating mental objects in mental objects internally, or he lives contemplating mental objects in mental objects externally, or he lives contemplating mental objects in mental objects internally and externally. He lives contemplating origination-factors in mental objects, or he lives contemplating dissolution-factors in mental objects, or he lives contemplating origination-and-dissolution-factors in mental objects. Or his mindfulness is established with the thought, "Mental objects exist," to the extent necessary just for knowledge and mindfulness, and he lives detached, and clings to naught in the world. Thus, monks, a monk lives contemplating mental objects in mental objects of the seven factors of enlightenment.

5. *The Four Noble Truths*

And further, monks, a monk lives contemplating mental objects in the mental objects of the four noble truths.

How monks, does a monk live contemplating mental objects in the mental objects of the four noble truths?

Herein, monks, a monk knows, "This is suffering," according to reality; he knows, "This is the origin of suffering," according to reality; he knows "This is the cessation of suffering," according to reality; he knows, "This is the road leading to the cessation of suffering," according to reality.

Thus he lives contemplating mental objects in mental objects internally, or he lives contemplating mental objects in mental objects externally, or he lives contemplating mental objects in mental objects internally and externally. He lives contemplating origination-factors in mental objects, or he lives contemplating dissolution-factors in mental objects, or he lives contemplating origination-and-dissolution-factors in mental objects. Or his mindfulness is established with the thought, "Mental objects exist," to the extent necessary just for knowledge and mindfulness, and he lives detached, and clings to naught in the world. Thus, monks, a monk lives contemplating mental objects in the mental objects of the four noble truths.

Verily, monks, whosoever practices these four Foundations of Mindfulness in this manner for seven years, then one of these two fruits may be expected by him: Highest Knowledge (Arhatship), here and now, or if some remainder of clinging is yet present, the state of Nonreturning.

O monks, let alone seven years. Should any person practicing these four Foundations of Mindfulness in this manner for six years . . . for five years . . . three years . . . two years . . . one year, then one of these two fruits may be expected by him: Highest Knowledge, here and now, or if some remainder of clinging is yet present, the state of Nonreturning.

O monks, let alone a year. Should any person practice these four Foundations on Mindfulness in this manner for seven months . . . for six months . . . five months . . . four months . . . three months . . . two months . . . a month . . . half a month, then one of these two fruits may be expected by him: Highest Knowledge, here and now, or if some remainder of clinging is yet present, the state of Nonreturning.

O monks, let alone half a month. Should any person practice these four Foundations of Mindfulness in this manner, for a week, then one of these two fruits may be expected by him: Highest Knowledge, here and now, or if some remainder of clinging is yet present, the state of Nonreturning.

Because of this it is said: "This is the only way, monks, for the purification of beings, for the overcoming of sorrow and lamentation, for the destruction of suffering and grief, for reaching the right path, for the attainment of Nirvāna, namely the four Foundations of Mindfulness."

Thus spoke the Blessed One. Satisfied, the monks approved of his words.

128

🏵 The Discourse on Mindfulness of Breathing

(Anāpānasati Sutta)

Translated from the Pali by Nyānaponika

Mindfulness of Breathing, monks, cultivated and regularly practiced, is of great fruit and great benefit. Mindfulness of Breathing, cultivated and regularly practiced, brings to Perfection the four Foundations of Mindfulness. The four Foundations of Mindfulness, cultivated and regularly practiced, bring the seven Factors of Enlightenment to perfection; the seven Factors of Enlightenment, cultivated and regularly practiced, bring wisdom and deliverance to perfection.

And how cultivated and regularly practiced, is Mindfulness of Breathing of great fruit and benefit?

Herein, monks, a monk having gone to the forest, to the foot of a tree, or to an empty place, sits down cross-legged, keeps his body erect and his mindfulness alert. Just mindful he breathes in, mindful he breathes out.

129

I. The First Tetrad (Contemplation of the Body)

1. Breathing in a long breath, he knows, "I breathe in a long breath"; breathing out a long breath, he knows, "I breathe out a long breath."

2. Breathing in a short breath, he knows, "I breathe in a short breath"; breathing out a short breath, he knows, "I breathe out a short breath."

3. "Experiencing the whole (breath-) body I shall breathe in," thus he trains himself; "Experiencing the whole (breath-) body I shall breathe out," thus he trains himself.

4. "Calming the bodily function (of breathing) I shall breathe in," thus he trains himself; "Calming the bodily function (of breathing) I shall breathe out," thus he trains himself.

II. The Second Tetrad (Contemplation of Feelings)

5. "Experiencing rapture I shall breathe in (I shall breathe out)," thus he trains himself.

6. "Experiencing happiness I shall breathe in (I shall breathe out)," thus he trains himself.

7. "Experiencing the mental functions I shall breathe in (I shall breathe out)," thus he trains himself.

8. "Calming the mental functions I shall breathe in (I shall breathe out)," thus he trains himself.

III. The Third Tetrad (Contemplation of the Mind)

9. "Experiencing the mind I shall breathe in (I shall breathe out)," thus he trains himself.

10. "Gladdening the mind I shall breathe in (I shall breathe out)," thus he trains himself.

11. "Concentrating the mind, I shall breathe in (I shall breathe out)," thus he trains himself.

12. "Liberating the mind I shall breathe in (I shall breathe out)," thus he trains himself.

IV. The Fourth Tetrad (Contemplation of Mind-objects)

13. "Contemplating impermanence I shall breathe in (I shall breathe out)," thus he trains himself.

14. "Contemplating dispassion I shall breathe in (I shall breathe out)," thus he trains himself.

15. "Contemplating cessation I shall breathe in (I shall breathe out)," thus he trains himself.

16. "Contemplating relinquishment I shall breathe in (I shall breathe out)," thus he trains himself.

17. In that way, cultivated and regularly practiced, monks, Mindfulness of Breathing brings great fruit and benefit.

Perfecting the Foundations of Mindfulness

And how cultivated, how regularly practiced brings Mindfulness of Breathing the four Foundations of Mindfulness to perfection?

I. Whenever a monk mindfully breathes in and out a long breath, or a short breath; or when he trains himself to breathe in and out while experiencing the bodily function (of breathing); or while calming that function—at that time, monks, he dwells practicing body-contemplation on the body, ardent, clearly comprehending, and mindful; having overcome covetousness and grief concerning the world. For, breathing in and out, monks, I say, is one of the bodily processes.

II. Whenever the monk trains himself to breathe in and out while experiencing rapture; or while experiencing happiness; or while experiencing the mental functions; or while calming the mental functions—at those times, monks, he dwells practicing feeling-contemplation on feelings, ardent, clearly comprehending, and mindful, having overcome covetousness and grief concerning the world. For the full attention to breathing in and out, I say, is one of the feelings.

III. Whenever a monk trains himself to breathe in and out while experiencing the mind; or while gladdening the mind; or while concentrating the mind; or while liberating the mind—at that time he dwells practicing mind-contemplation on the mind, ardent, clearly comprehending, and mindful, having overcome covetousness and grief concerning the world. For one who lacks mindfulness and clear comprehension, I say, cannot develop Mindfulness of Breathing.

IV. Whenever a monk trains himself to breathe in and out while contemplating impermanence, dispassion, cessation, or relinquishment—at that time he dwells practicing mind-object contemplation on mind-objects, ardent, clearly comprehending, and mindful, having overcome covetousness and grief concerning the world. Having wisely seen the abandoning of covetousness and grief, he looks on with perfect equanimity.

Mindfulness of Breathing, monks, in that way cultivated and regularly practiced, brings the four Foundations of Mindfulness to perfection.

And how do the four Foundations cultivated and regularly practiced, bring the seven Factors of Enlightenment to perfection?

Whenever a monk dwells in the contemplation of

body, feelings, mind, and mind-objects, ardent . . . unclouded mindfulness becomes established in him. And when unclouded mindfulness is established in him, at that time the enlightenment-factor "Mindfulness" is initiated in the monk; at that time the monk develops the enlightenment-factor Mindfulness; at that time he gains perfection in the development of the enlightenment-factor "Mindfulness."

Dwelling mindful in that manner, he wisely investigates, examines, and scrutinizes the respective object; and while doing so, the enlightenment-factor "Investigation of Reality" is initiated in the monk; at that time the monk develops the enlightenment-factor "Investigation of Reality"; at that time he gains perfection in the development of the enlightenment-factor "Investigation of Reality."

While he wisely investigates, examines, and scrutinizes that object, unremitting energy is initiated in him. And when the unremitting factor "Energy" is initiated in him, at that time the monk develops the enlightenment-factor "Energy"; at that time he gains perfection in the development of the enlightenment-factor "Energy."

In him possessed of energy unworldly rapture arises. And when in a monk possessed of energy unworldly rapture arises, at that time the enlightenment-factor "Rapture" is initiated in him; at that time the monk develops the enlightenment-factor "Rapture"; at that time the monk gains perfection in the development of the enlightenment-factor "Rapture."

The body and mind of one who is filled with rapture become tranquil. And when the body and mind of one who is filled with rapture become tranquil, at that time the enlightenment-factor "Tranquility" is initiated in him; at that time the monk develops the en-lightenment-factor "Tranquility."

The mind of one who is tranquil and happy becomes concentrated. And when the mind of a monk who is tranquil and happy becomes concentrated, at that time the enlightenment-factor "Concentration" is initiated in him; at that time the monk develops the enlightenment-factor "Concentration"; at that time he gains perfection in the development of the enlighten-ment-factor "Concentration."

On the mind thus concentrated he looks with per-fect equanimity. And when looking on his concen-trated mind with perfect equanimity, at that time the enlightenment factor "Equanimity" is initiated in him; at that time the monk develops the enlightenment-factor "Equanimity"; at that time he gains perfection in the development of the enlightenment-factor "Equanimity."

The four Foundations of Mindfulness, in that way cultivated and regularly practiced, bring the seven Fac-tors of Enlightenment to perfection.

And how do the seven Factors of Enlightenment, cultivated and regularly practiced, bring wisdom and deliverance to perfection?

Herein, monks, a monk develops the enlighten-ment-factors Mindfulness, Investigation of Reality, En-ergy, Rapture, Tranquility, Concentration, and Equanimity, based on detachment, based on dispas-sion, based on cessation, resulting in relinquishment.

The seven Factors of Enlightenment, in that way cultivated and regularly practiced, bring wisdom and deliverance to perfection.

Thus spoke the Exalted One. Glad in heart the monks rejoiced in the words of the Blessed One.

134

🏵 Contemplation of Thought

From Siksāsamuccaya

Translated from the Sanskrit by Edward Conze

He searches all around for his thought. But what thought? It is either passionate, or hateful, or confused. What about the past, future, or present? What is past that is extinct, what is future that has not yet arrived, and the present has no stability. For thought, Kasyapa, cannot be apprehended, inside, or outside, or in between both. For thought is immaterial, invisible, nonresisting, inconceivable, unsupported, and homeless. Thought has never been seen by any of the Buddhas, nor do they see it, nor will they see it. And what the Buddhas never see, how can that be an observable process, except in the sense that dharmas proceed by the way of mistaken perception? Thought is like a magical illusion; by an imagination of what is actually unreal it takes hold of a manifold variety of rebirths. A thought is like the stream of a river, without any staying power; as soon as it is produced it breaks up and disappears. A thought is like the flame of a lamp, and it proceeds through causes and conditions. A thought is like lightning, it breaks up in a moment and does not stay on. . . .

Searching for thought all round, he does not see it within or without. He does not see it in the skandhas, or in the elements, or in the sense-fields. Unable to see thought, he seeks to find the trend of thought, and asks himself: Whence is the genesis of thought? And it occurs to him that "where there is an object, there thought arises." Is then the thought one thing, and the object another? No, what is the object, just that is the thought. If the object were one thing, and the thought another, then there would be a double state of thought. So the object itself is just thought. Can then thought review thought? No, thought cannot review thought. As the blade of a sword cannot cut itself, so a thought cannot see itself. Moreover, vexed and pressed hard on all sides, thought proceeds, without any staying power, like a monkey or like the wind. It ranges far, bodiless, easily changing, agitated by the objects of sense, with the six sense-fields for its sphere, connected with one thing after another. The stability of thought, its one-pointedness, its immobility, its undistraughtness, its one-pointed calm, its nondistraction, that is on the other hand called mindfulness as to thought.

❀ Not Dwelling on the Nonconditioned

From the Vimalakirtinirdesa Sutra

Translated from the Chinese by Nhat Hanh

What does it mean, "not dwelling on the Nonconditioned"? The bodhisattva contemplates the reality of Emptiness but does not take Emptiness as an object of attainment. The bodhisattva practices the reality of Nonappearance and Nonpursuit but does not take Nonappearance or Nonpursuit as an object of attainment. He contemplates the reality of Noncreation but does not take Noncreation as an object of attainment. He meditates on the truth of Impermanence but does not abandon his work to serve and save. He meditates on Suffering but does not reject the world of births and deaths. He meditates on Extinction but does not embrace Extinction. He meditates on Detachment but goes on realizing good things in the world. He meditates on the homeless nature of dharmas but continues to orientate himself toward the Good. He meditates on the reality of Neither-creation-nor-destruction but still undertakes the responsibility in the world of creations and destructions. He meditates on the reality of the

Ultimate but still dwells in the world of interdependent origins. He meditates on Nonaction but continues always his acts of service and education. He meditates on Emptiness but does not abandon Great Compassion. He meditates on the Position of the True Dharma but does not follow a rigid path. He meditates on the Unreal, Impermanent, Unoriginated, Nonpossessed, and Markless nature of dharmas but does not abandon his career concerning merits, concentration, and wisdom. Practicing in that way, the bodhisattva is described as "not dwelling on the Nonconditioned." He has wisdom but does not end his action in the realm of the conditioned; he has compassion but does not dwell in the Nonconditioned; he wants to realize his great Vow but he will not abandon the conditioned world.

❀ The Heart of the Prajñāpāramitā

Translated from the Chinese by Nhat Hanh

The bodhisattva Avalokita, while moving in the deep course of the Perfect Wisdom, shed light on the five aggregates and found them equally empty. After this penetration, he overcame all pain.

"Listen, Sāriputra, form is emptiness, emptiness is form, form does not differ from emptiness, emptiness does not differ from form. The same thing is true with feeling, perception, mental functioning, and consciousness.

"Here, Sāriputra, all dharmas are marked with emptiness; they are neither produced nor destroyed, neither defiled nor immaculate, neither increasing nor decreasing. Therefore, in emptiness there is neither form, nor feeling, nor perception, nor mental functioning, nor consciousness; no eye, or ear, or nose, or tongue, or body, or mind; no form, no sound, no smell, no taste, no touchable, no object of mind, no realm of elements (from sight to mind-consciousness), no interdependent origins (from ignorance to death and decay), no extinction of death and decay, no suffering, no origination of suffering, no extinction, no path, no wisdom, no attainment.

"Because there is no attainment, the bodhisattva, basing on the Perfection of Wisdom, finds no obstacles for his mind. Having no obstacles, he overcomes fear, liberating himself forever from illusion and assault and realizing perfect Nirvāna. All Buddhas in the past, present, and future, thanks to this Perfect Wisdom, arrive to full, right, and universal Enlightenment.

"Therefore one should know that the Perfect Wisdom is a great mantra, is the highest mantra, is the unequaled mantra, the destroyer of all suffering, the incorruptible truth. A mantra of Prajñāpāramitā should therefore be proclaimed. It is this: 'Gone, gone, gone to the other shore, gone together to the other shore. O Awakening! All hail!' "